ABOLISHING WAR

Cultures and Institutions

Dialogue with peace scholars
ELISE BOULDING *and*
RANDALL FORSBERG

To Landrum,
In celebration of your
adventurous 85 year journey
to make the world more peaceful!
With much love,
Elise Boulding
11-16-98

**BOSTON RESEARCH CENTER
FOR THE 21ST CENTURY**

November 1998

The **Boston Research Center for the 21st Century** (BRC) is an international peace institute founded in 1993 by Daisaku Ikeda, a Buddhist peace activist and president of Soka Gakkai International, an association of Buddhist organizations in 128 countries. The BRC brings together scholars and activists in dialogue on common values across cultures and religions, seeking in this way to support an evolving global ethic for a peaceful twenty-first century. Human rights, nonviolence, ecological harmony, and economic justice are focal points of the Center's work.

Published by
Boston Research Center for the 21st Century
396 Harvard Street
Cambridge, MA 02138-3924

ISBN 1-887917-03-9
Library of Congress catalogue card number: 98-074360

© 1998 Boston Research Center for the 21st Century

Edited by Helen Marie Casey and Amy Morgante
Copyediting by Kali Saposnick
Desktop publishing and cover design by Ralph Buglass
Abolishing War seminar series organized by Karen Nardella and
    Beth Zimmerman

TABLE OF CONTENTS

Preface

From time immemorial, the story of humankind is a story of conflict and the resolution of conflict. Sometimes, in fact, it has seemed that the history of the world has been a history of war. Yet those who have been on battlefields have ended by decrying war. "War is at best barbarism," William Tecumseh Sherman said in 1879. "It is only those who have neither fired a shot nor heard the shrieks and groans of the wounded who cry aloud for blood, more vengeance, more desolation. War is hell."

From its founding, the Boston Research Center for the 21st Century has devoted all of its energy to the promotion of peace. Toward that end, during the past year, the BRC sponsored a series of seminars on the abolition of war in which peace activists Elise Boulding and Randall Forsberg—both Global Citizens—met together in dialogue to examine the strategies that might effect the end of war.

They proposed workable approaches, looked for the weaknesses in the arguments that each offered, and came together time and time again in an effort to see more clearly what is needed to change individual thinking, individual behavior, and the institutions that attend to the making of war.

These two strategists for peace, in concert with seminar participants, evolved quite different but complementary approaches to the question: How shall we bring an end to war? The BRC is publishing the dialogues of Dr. Boulding and Dr. Forsberg, comments from participants, and invited commentaries in order to share the richness of the ideas communicated over a period of half a dozen months with a larger community of citizens concerned with peace and peacemaking.

In his autobiography, Nelson Mandela observed: "Time and again, I have seen men and women risk and give their lives for an idea." It is our hope that the ideas contained in this text will circulate widely, engender enthusiasm, and make a difference.

—*Virginia Straus*
Executive Director
Boston Research Center for the 21st Century

Foreword

When the pantheon of significant figures who contributed to the dismantling of the war system is chronicled by historians in the middle of the twenty-first century, Elise Boulding and Randall Forsberg will undoubtedly be in the first tier. Their commitment, competence, and scholarly and analytic contributions, combined with their involvement in political action, have been extraordinary. Each of them has been innovative and creative in identifying fundamental ways of thinking and acting in this domain.

Presented in a conversational style, Boulding's and Forsberg's essays contain pithy and illuminating basic formulations on how to think about and act within the movement to abolish war. The essays are further enhanced by the written comments of the distinguished participants who were involved in the seminar series, "The Conditions for Abolishing War: Cultures and Institutions," organized by the Boston Research Center. The contrasting and complementary perspectives of Boulding (understanding and creating a culture of peace) and Forsberg (understanding and designing a program focusing specifically on the security and military area) add information, analyses, and rich interpretation, which provide depth and solidity to what is known—as well as highlighting issues which bear further discussion.

This volume, then, will undoubtedly be useful for courses on conflict resolution and peace and world order studies in universities throughout the world. In addition, the essays possess shrewd insights linking scholarly materials to contemporary political, social, and cultural life, as well as security and military matters. Thus, the policy community would be well advised to study these materials for they contain significant initiatives which officialdom could begin to undertake to promote the abolition of war.

And the abolition of war is in the offing. That is to say, wherever one locates the historical origin point(s) of this momentous and magnificent movement, it is clear that despite, or perhaps more to the point, because of the horrors of war, genocide, and other deadly conflicts of this century, the necessary elements for a regime abolishing war are finally taking place. Aggressive war, genocide, and crimes against humanity have been criminalized. Individual responsibility has been affixed for these crimes. The Nuremberg and Tokyo tribunals following World War II laid the authoritative foundation for outlawing crimes against peace (aggression), war crimes, and crimes against humanity. The genocide treaty, the codification of the Nuremberg code, the four Geneva Conventions of 1949, the protocols of 1977, scholarly and policy officialdom discussions of these matters over the past four decades, and the two international criminal courts for former Yugoslavia and Rwanda reflect a painstakingly slow, but nevertheless irreversible, process in this regard. The treaty calling for the creation of a permanent international criminal court has been adopted by an overwhelming number of the states of the world, albeit the United States and others (i.e., China, Iraq, Libya) are being brought into this process very reluctantly. Furthermore, the sense here is that police forces to prevent, apprehend, and carry out judicial sentences are only a decade away. Legislative capacity, either through treaty and/or binding General Assembly resolutions, creating and maintaining a global polity of a world without war, is also within a two-decade horizon.

These projections (some might label them prophetics) are touched upon, but not explored, in this text. I do not wish to presume that Boulding and Forsberg necessarily concur with them. I want now to touch upon three other fledgling and putative opportunities: specie identity, global citizenship, and world government.

Specie identity. The notion that each human being has the capacity to identify with the human race as well as the particular group into which one has been socialized is what is meant by specie identity. At a minimum, we should ask the questions: Do we need a critical mass of individuals throughout the globe who are actualizing specie identity and wish to manifest this identity within the context of delegitimizing and dismantling the war system? Stated as a political and social proposition (hypothesis), a cadre of some 20 to 30 percent of the human race who manifest specie identity would provide a critical mass for the movement to dismantle the war system. What needs to be noted here is that this critical mass has been emerging over the past three decades. Not so far below the surface of behavior and attitudes, participants and actors in the environment, human rights, anti-apartheid, basic needs, and feminist movements have been exercising specie identity. That is to say, they have been arguing their cause on the principle that each human being is entitled to minimal decency standards. We need now to articulate the ethical and psychological underpinnings of specie identity of these movements so that groups and individuals throughout the globe are fully aware of the presence and potency of this identity. The exercise of specie identity does not comprehend suppressing identities already opposed or professed, i.e., gender, family, religion, society, or polity. Nor does it privilege specie identity as the fundamental or supreme matrix of humanity. Specie identity does, however, allow and encourage the intertwining of our feelings of common humanity with our more particular membership identities.

Global citizenship. Furthermore, the articulation of specie identity suggests the possibility, and even necessity, of global citizenship. That is to say, as more and more individuals throughout the world claim the planet as the territory to which they belong and claim a set of principles that clearly states minimum decency standards for the 6.5 billion human beings circa 2010, the call for global citizenship as a status within human polity is likely to become a major social force. One way in which this force will be manifested leads to the notion of world government.

World government. Governance is a term which has been used by social scientists to account for the way individuals and groups exercise social control throughout society. Thus, governance points to the institutions, organizations, and processes, including family, peer groups, religion, workplace, as well as the political organization of the state and the globe. This web of connectedness establishes normative standards, allocates resources, deals with conflicts, and orders class and status patterns as well as other institutions and organizations of human society. At the same time, in using the terminology of "governance," many individuals and groups active in the political arena are consciously distancing themselves from the term "government." (See, for example, the publication, *Our Global Neighborhood*, of the prestigious and distinguished Commission on Global Governance.) This pro-governance posture has its roots in both preference and feasibility. As to preference, there is the view that world government would be undesirable; world government curtails and limits national sovereignty. Beyond that, world government could become a totalitarian state oppressive to humankind. Secondly, given the political realities of contemporary society, there is a lack of political will to achieve world government; in short, even if desirable, it is not feasible. It is utopian. The possibility of world government becoming a totalitarian state is, of course, always there.

But if one reviews the emergence of democratic polities and human rights throughout the globe over the past two centuries, it is fair to say that human society has had significant experience in preventing—or in extreme circumstances dislodging—dictatorships. We have only to look at the former Soviet Union and Latin America, as well as stirrings in the People's Republic of China and elsewhere, for evidence of this trend. Government accountability and response to electorates are increasingly becoming the norm, however ragged progress is in this area. Within this *accountability* of government, the rule of law is an essential element. Executive power and legislative capacity rest on electoral processes and review by independent judiciaries. Tyranny and dictatorship are perennial matters of government, but need not occur.

Furthermore, the rule of law at this moment in history is inextricably interwoven with government, and government is needed as the formal authority structure to deal with conflicts and violence. The same is likely to be true for the prevention of war, genocide, and other deadly conflicts throughout the globe. To be sure, other forms of governance are important, but government is an essential component of governance structures and without government we are unlikely to abolish war.

The sovereignty problematique runs across the full spectrum of substantive domains—political, economic, social, and security. At the same time it is clear, as Boutros Boutros-Ghali pointed out "that the time of absolute and exclusive sovereignty has passed; its theory was never matched by reality" (*An Agenda for Peace* 1995). In this interdependent and interpenetrative world, national elite decision-making has had to accommodate more and more to financial, investment, information, cultural, and religious belief flows, as well as other governments. The sovereignty of the state to determine its own defense structure has also been altered. Indeed, when states no longer need to rely on their own defense structures—that is, when a world authority maintaining peace and security is in place—the release of material and human resources will increase the sovereignty of individuals. As it is, defense and security issues, as they run the spectrum from military budgets to the garrison states, curtail the sovereignty of people.

The feasibility issue is best explored within the context of historical trends that are taking place. Most analyses of the contemporary global political scene fix the post-Cold War and the phenomenon of globalization as the frame for description and evaluation. At the same time, there is a good deal of contestation in the interpretation of these events for the near and intermediate future. One needs only to refer to the following authors and their work: Fukyama, *The End of History;* Huntington, *The Clash of Civilizations;* Grieder, *One World or None, The Manic Logic of Capitalism;* Kaplan, *The Coming Anarchy;* Kothari, *The World Adrift.* Our reading of these and other authors concerned with these matters reveals a major omission in depicting the present global circumstances. While a number of these works recognize the emergence of transnational civil society, they underestimate the extent to which there is a movement or a set of movements promoting a just world order. This is a world in which the delegitimizing and dismantling of aggressive war, genocide, and other deadly conflicts have become a focus for social and political action, as witness The Hague Appeal for Peace Convocation for May 1999. The movement(s) demands basic needs for every human being on the face of the globe, minimal standards of social justice, and ecological equilibrium for the planet. The argument here is that the movement to abolish war has roots in these various efforts and that the normative progress which has taken place in these areas will soon be matched by organizational and institutional expression.

Coda. To think, feel, and act as a global citizen is an essential requirement for the study of, and participation in, the movement to abolish war and establish a just world order. Elise Boulding and Randall Forsberg have provided us wise guidance on the path to achieving these goals.

—Saul Mendlovitz
Dag Hammarskjold Professor
Peace and World Order Studies
Rutgers Law School

11
.
.
.
.
.

SEMINAR #1

Toward the Abolition of War: Trends and Prospects

BY RANDALL FORSBERG

Introduction

I'm delighted that you're all here and appreciate the opportunity to exchange ideas about the conditions under which war could end. I'm grateful to Elise Boulding for having invited me to share the opportunity to participate in this series with her and to the Boston Research Center for initiating and hosting the series.

The purpose of these seminars is to conduct a dialogue between two broadly conceived approaches to the possibility of abolishing war, one focusing primarily on individuals and changes in individual values, behavior, and activities, the other focusing mainly on the state and changes in government policy and state-to-state behavior. These two approaches are represented by my presentations on the state side and Elise's work on the culture of peace on the individual side.

People who take the state-oriented approach tend to think that approaches which stress the values and behavior of individuals are fully complementary and essential for the success of the state-oriented approach. Unfortunately, those who focus on the culture of peace or the individual-oriented approach often seem not to see the usefulness of government-oriented activity. In fact, in many cases those who stress change in individual values and behavior see government-oriented approaches as a waste of time or even counterproductive with respect to the key developments needed to end war.

From my point of view then, the purpose of this series is twofold: first, to enrich my own thinking about both approaches by sharing ideas; and secondly, more narrowly, to try to convince those of you who favor the individual-oriented approach that some government-oriented activities can be reconciled with and form a key component of a more effective integrative strategy, which also addresses change in individual values and behavior.

The reason for underscoring the divergence between the two approaches is that one major difference between them has long obstructed and weakened efforts for peace. That divisive issue concerns commitment to exclusively nonviolent means of working for a world without war.

The question of whether there are any circumstances in which the use of armed force (or explicit support for the potential use of armed force) may be helpful in moving toward a world without war is one on which people have deeply-held beliefs and strong feelings. The issue goes to the heart of efforts to abolish war since, in the view of some, it is the first principle of such efforts: What we really need in order to abolish war, they argue, is for enough individuals to realize that war is *always* wrong and unnecessary— and then to find ways of going about our business without resorting to war. This approach imbues not only the work of explicitly pacifist organizations but also the activities of many anti-nuclear and other peace groups. Often, these groups prioritize cuts in particular weapons as a day-to-day tactic, even though they believe that there are no morally acceptable weapons or military strategies. Peace Action (the successor organization to the Nuclear Weapons Freeze Campaign and SANE), for example, generally takes this view.

Others believe with equal conviction, as I do, that complete renunciation of the use of armed force in all situations is much less likely to lead to world peace than is the establishment of an international counterpart to national governments—a reformed U.N. which is empowered to use armed force to deter and quell deadly force. The view that providing for military defense is necessary but can be reconciled with efforts for peace and disarmament is common among those who focus on international institutions, such as the United Nations or regional security organizations, among World Federalists, and in many mainstream liberal or social democratic organizations.

My hope in this seminar series is to try to bridge the seemingly unbridgeable gap between these two perspectives, or at least to create a better appreciation on each side of the thinking on the other side, and to establish some common ground for effective collaboration.

"Least-Change" Conditions for Peace

Let me begin by taking a broad view of the question of the conditions for the abolition of war, and by making some formal distinctions. Logically, in considering what would have to happen to abolish war, we can identify different kinds of conditions; for example, (1) conditions *conducive* to the abolition of war, (2) conditions *necessary* for the abolition of war, and (3) conditions *sufficient* for the abolition of war.

The "culture of peace" approach is concerned with conditions conducive to the abolition of war. In this approach, one looks across the broad range of diverse conditions in society, culture, and political institutions, and tries to identify conditions which would be helpful in the effort to abolish war, that is, conditions which would help generate other conditions which may be necessary for peace. For example, many people believe that the removal of violence from children's television programming would be conducive to the development in children of the moral values and patterns of behavior that are necessary to the creation of a peaceful world.

My approach looks at the opposite end of the spectrum of conditions for abolition. I have tried to identify the *least change* that would be necessary in Western society, and globally, for war to be abolished. Clearly, many things would be conducive to the abolition of war, such as the achievement of a much greater degree of economic welfare throughout the world, in both the rich and the poor countries; more equity in income, education, and opportunity; a healthy natural environment; and improved skills for nonviolent resolution of conflicts. But it has seemed to me that it would facilitate the goal if we ask, What is the *sine qua non*? What must happen, at a minimum, in order for peace to be established?

After long study, I concluded that a single, modest change could serve as a catalyst to somewhat broader (but still relatively limited) changes which, in turn, could lead to the initial abolition of war and, ultimately, the permanent abolition of war. That single modest change is the development of a commitment in a great majority of the public to the democratic value that violence is *never* morally or politically acceptable except when used in defense against its use by others who have not accepted this principle and have initiated acts of violence.

15
.
.
.
.
.

This criterion for the use of violence or armed force differs from the traditional "just war" view that the use of violence is acceptable if the means are proportionate to the ends and the ends are just. Under the defense-oriented rule that I propose, there are *no* just *proactive* uses of violence or force. There is only one just use, and that is the limited reactive purpose of trying to stop and reverse the harm being done by those who have not accepted that there are no just uses of force.

An important feature of the "defense-only" version of the just war approach is that if everyone were genuinely committed to never use armed force except in defense against its use by others, there would be no war.

I call commitment never to use violence or armed force except in defense "belief in defensive nonviolence." (I previously used the phrase "commitment to nonviolence" but my friend, international relations scholar Hayward Alker, urged me to avoid the appearance of trying to usurp the use of this phrase from those who are already using it to mean commitment to nonviolence with no exceptions. "Defensive nonviolence" is a poor substitute since it employs a misplaced modifier, but it does convey the intended sense: *No violence except for defense.*) Those who apply this standard strictly may be as fully committed to nonviolence as those who are committed to no violence under any circumstances because the key to belief in nonviolence is one's view about situations in which it is just to *initiate* violence. Those who believe in defensive nonviolence, like those who believe in complete nonviolence, are convinced that there are no situations in which initiating violence is justified or acceptable.

I believe that, without any other major changes in culture, politics, or economics, a shift from an already widespread belief in defensive nonviolence to a *predominant* belief in this value could lead to a world without war. In the first stage of what will inevitably be a decades-long process of change, predominant popular belief in the importance of confining the use of armed force to defense, strictly and narrowly conceived, would tend to preclude the initiation of the use of force on the part of the governments involved; and that, in turn, would help decrease the incidence of war.

Then, in the second and final stage of change, the combination of (1) cultural commitment never to use force except in defense,

(2) government policies structured to oppose the use of armed force except for defense, narrowly defined, and (3) the declining frequency of war, taken together, would be likely to foster the growth of a more far-reaching commitment to nonviolence—a commitment comparable or identical to that among ardent pacifists.

This more far-reaching commitment, gradually spreading around the world, would allow the establishment of an enduring peace in which, even under conditions of great pressure and stress, political institutions established to keep the peace would endure and succeed.

The Concept of "Defensive Nonviolence" and Its Application in U.S. Foreign and Military Policy

I began thinking about the "least-change" route to the abolition of war in the mid-1970s, when I asked myself, What are the obstacles to the growth of norms and institutions that would permit the establishment of a lasting peace?

One obvious obstacle at that time was the mistrust and fear of war between East and West that was being fueled by the large size, offensive potential, and ever-improving technology of the armed forces on both sides. Since the "technological" arms race is so obviously costly and detrimental to confidence in the peace and to the development of positive relations, why don't governments try harder to stop it? I wondered. What obstacle prevents governments from undertaking to eliminate or minimize the *military* sources of fear and hostility, which of all sources of mistrust are most readily susceptible to government intervention and change?

Studying U.S. military and arms control policy with this question in mind, I discovered that the kinds of forces that the United States had used in Vietnam were not introduced temporarily for the purpose of that war but were a permanent part of U.S. forces in peace time. It was U.S. policy to maintain permanently in peacetime the military capability to intervene in civil wars and lesser conflicts in the Third World to promote the establishment of governments that were to the liking of the U.S. government.

Prior to this discovery I had assumed that the purpose of U.S. peacetime military policy and forces was to be prepared to defend the United States, or, if not the United States, other countries such

17
.
.
.
.
.

as the countries of Europe, from external aggression by a militarily powerful country, such as the Soviet Union. In other words, I had assumed that the role of U.S. armed forces was strictly defensive. By comparison with the strictly defensive role I had imagined, intervening militarily in internal conflicts in other nations in order to determine the outcome of those conflicts is much less defensive, much more a traditional great power use of force. It means employing the greater wealth of a large, developed nation, and the superior military power that wealth can buy, to influence the course of political developments outside that nation's borders.

The moment I realized that part of U.S. peacetime military policy was to be prepared for military intervention in conflicts within smaller, militarily weaker countries, I understood why governments did not view arms control and disarmament as a way to build confidence and strengthen peace. If two great powers—the U.S. and the former U.S.S.R.—maintain armed forces not because they want to defend mutually but because they are interested in using force in situations where they can get away with it and just want to make sure that force is not used against them—in other words, they want to be sure that they can use armed force with impunity—then we certainly can't achieve either disarmament or a stable, disarmed peace. We can't achieve these goals, first, because governments don't want peace with disarmament; they want to keep open the option to use armed force pro-actively in certain situations. Secondly, because in a world of self-interested military interventions, each side is right to doubt the motives, sincerity, and ability to follow though on commitments made in disarmament talks with the other side.

I concluded that continuing acceptance by decision-making elites of an eighteenth- or nineteenth-century view of the role of armed force in the international system is the *foremost* obstacle to the abolition of war, but an obstacle which is being overlooked or ignored by peace groups. This aspect of government policy is not criticized outright, not taken on directly. And probably an important reason for this is that those most passionately committed to peace don't want to argue about legitimate and illegitimate or moral and immoral uses of force, or even make distinctions of that kind in their own thinking and analysis. As a result, the people who do argue about military strategy, and make military strategy, are those who believe that the war system is going to be with us forever. This perpetuates self-interested uses of force.

Initial Commitment to Defensive Nonviolence and the Development of Unalterable Commitment to Nonviolence

As I started developing the thesis that if nations stuck to defense we could build a bridge to a peaceful, disarmed world, I rechecked for arguments among mainstream security analysts and international relations scholars to see whether there was anything that I had overlooked which would negate the thesis. Was I forgetting something? Were there any additional profound obstacles to peace apart from tolerance of the use of armed force as an instrument of government policy?

I found one important obstacle to peace that was not addressed by this remedy (limiting the use of armed force to defense, narrowly defined). This is the expectation that when placed under sufficient stress, all political institutions, including institutions designed to keep the peace, tend to collapse. No government, no system of political organization, has ever survived the worst onslaughts of economic deprivation, catastrophe, or even dislocation due to profound changes in other nearby areas.

In thinking about the abolition of war, I was trying to envisage a situation in which so-called "rogue" states would never arise—that is, not merely a situation in which the majority of people and countries would be defensive in values and policy, but a situation in which the need for military defenses would ultimately disappear and could then reasonably be expected never to arise again. This would mean the establishment of a genuinely stable, permanent peace, not just a temporary, unstable peace.

(In this connection, a scholar named Stark who worked at the Polemological Institute in Holland in the 1960s made a similar distinction between establishing and perpetuating peace. But Stark takes the opposite view: He treats peace as the normal condition and war as the aberrant condition. As a result, his first question is how to preserve peace, while his second question is how to restore peace when it's been broken. In my approach, the first step is establishing peace and later steps perpetuate it.)

Accepting that political institutions tend to collapse when placed under sufficient stress—in other words, the possibility that under adverse future conditions, one or another nation or group, which was suffering, could become militarily aggressive—I asked myself whether there were any conditions under which even during extreme stress, war would not break out. If no such conditions could be identified, I thought, this might create a prohibitive obstacle to peace because even if the fatal collapse never happened, government leaders could persuasively argue that it is unwise to disarm because sooner or later such aggression will occur. In other words, there will never be a situation in which we can safely live without reliance on armed force: we can never establish a genuinely stable, fully disarmed world peace.

Is it possible to imagine a world in which people might be under great pressure, but war simply wouldn't occur to them as a possible reaction because it would have become an unthinkable form of behavior?

We do, in fact, have a history of human experience involving uses of violence which were, at one time, socially sanctioned and then became outlawed and then became unthinkable. The activities included in this category are:

- First, ritual cannibalism, which it turns out was probably very widely practiced among the simplest societies. Possibly 50 percent of all of these societies had some form of consumption of some piece of an enemy or piece of a relative as part of their spiritual life.
- Second, human sacrifice seems to have been universally practiced by all of the great ancient civilizations.
- Third, there is also slavery, which has been extremely widely practiced in all parts of the world throughout history.
- Finally, there have been extremely violent forms of physical punishment for law breaking: drawing and quartering, which meant that ropes were tied to people's hands and feet with horses attached to them; people were literally pulled apart as a punishment for some crime. There was the rack, burning at the stake, and so on.

All of these types of violence have now not only been outlawed, but also, for the most part, in most places, they are simply unthinkable forms of human behavior.

People tend to react to this argument by saying, "Well, that's beside the point because people used to think that cannibalism and human sacrifice achieved something, but we no longer think of those practices as means to an end. War is definitely a means to an end. You conquer, you take over, you get territory, and so on. So there's a really important distinction." But I don't think there is. The point is: In that future world, it would become apparent that what you can accomplish with war has no bearing on the crisis at hand. In fact, there is no crisis that can't be made worse by war.

The idea is that if you could create a world in which war is beyond the pale—one of those barbaric things that people used to do in ancient times for reasons which at the time they believed in very deeply and passionately—people will feel that whatever the problems are, war is not part of the answer.

I see this as a two-step process of moral change. The first step is a commitment never to use armed force except for defense. This is a pathway or a bridge to a second step in which the whole concept of war becomes as revolting as the concept of cannibalism is to us today, something that we can't really believe that people ever did to each other. In our culture it is so deeply ingrained that eating a piece of another human being is a horror beyond conception that we just physically can't imagine ourselves making the motions that would end up with human consumption. The thought makes us feel paralyzed.

Imagine a world in which people feel that way about war. The typical response to the very idea of war would be: "What is this? You're going to take young people and send them out and dismember and kill them—and then you're going to call them heroes, and you're going to decide something or other by means of this vicious, brutal, totally inhuman process? That doesn't make any sense."

In a sense, then, the culture of peace is what I, too, am talking about. The difference is that I'm focusing not on the end state but on a bridge for getting beyond the division in our thought and working for peace.

Prospects for Predominant Commitment to Defensive Nonviolence

Now let me look at how plausible this route is and how it might work. The concept of a democratic state or democratic governance is that you decide things by talking about them instead of by using force. That is the distinction between the secular representative governments introduced in the last several hundred years and the governments based on church or arbitrary hierarchies of power with kings or emperors, both of which used force. In a democracy, the idea is that nobody is "brought into line" by the use of force; everyone gets to participate in the decision-making, and force is not required.

The spread of democracy and the spread of the view that individuals have dignity and worth have been associated over the last several hundred years with a general trend away from socially-sanctioned forms of violence and toward the view that there is never any acceptable use of violence except for defense.

There are many examples of the movement away from socially-sanctioned violence, including: training women to defend themselves; the banning of spanking children; the elimination of beating children in school; the abolition of public hangings and of killing people by inflicting torturous punishment or by burning; and the movement to abolish the death penalty. All of these successive changes which have occurred over the last two or three centuries exemplify changes which I think reflect one central value: Every individual has worth and dignity and, therefore, no individual should ever be assaulted.

It's very hard, however, to apply this concept of defensive nonviolence to activities in the international system, for several reasons. Generally, we know that in our culture and in others, there are regressive attitudes that remain toward "out groups" and others who are considered different. That is still a major problem.

Foreign policy tends to be an elite-run activity which the average person is willing to leave to the specialists with the view that, "It's not my business. I don't know whose it is but someone is taking care of it, and it's certainly not mine." If you don't call the shots politically, then obviously you don't call them morally either. That makes it very hard to have these non-violent values translated into the foreign policy area.

For many people, the problem with the idea of defensive military policies is less an objection in principle than a problem of practice. Historical experience suggests that recognizing any "just" use of violence is like a slippery slope or like the circus clown's unending handkerchief: You start with one exception and then, as you keep pulling, new exceptions appear which end up rationalizing *all* uses of violence. The problem with the defense-only principle is, thus, that what is defensive is not sufficiently well defined or well agreed to for this to be a useful stricture or a meaningful limit. We know that governments tend to justify every military action on the grounds of being defensive, and populations tend to think that their own country's use of force is defensive while others' uses are aggressive.

Further, in international affairs, there are society-wide and trans-border disputes which have long histories that go over many generations, which make it impossible to determine if a given act of violence is defensive or offensive. In fact, the end of the great power war system and the transition to ethnic and border conflicts as the largest conflicts in the world represents a positive step but a difficult step. The more obviously aggressive uses of force are in the process of ending, but the more ambiguous and intractable historical cases of back-and-forth violence and retribution are the ones that we are now faced with. These are far more difficult to end following this principle of defensive nonviolence than are great power interventions in small Third World countries.

Finally, in the international system, the ideal is: You try not to kill, you try not to harm, you try to interpose and to end conflict and to defuse conflict. Ideally, that should be the role of the international community in a defensively-oriented world security system: trying to enforce the non-use of force, except for defense and to aid in defense. But it's virtually impossible for the international community to use armed force in this way in these kinds of intractable domestic conflicts—that is, to avoid hurting the innocent, to avoid becoming ensnared in the perpetuation of the conflict, to avoid taking sides, and finally, and perhaps most important, to keep from appropriating the responsibility for the ultimate political resolution of the conflict, which can only be accomplished by the parties involved, and not by outside intervening military powers.

In spite of these negative conditions at home, there are several positive developments in the international system that I'm sure you're familiar with. I'll just mention them briefly. With the end of the Cold War, we've moved into a period in which major conventional war with large-scale conventional aggression on the part of one country against another is extremely unlikely to happen and is widely believed to be extremely unlikely to happen.

It's unfortunate that that period was introduced by Iraq's aggression against Kuwait—almost the first such case of large-scale outright military aggression since World War II. This totally undermined or obscured people's ability to see that we're moving into a different period. And there is still a concern with risks of war between the Koreas, between India and Pakistan, in the Middle East, and with China and Taiwan.

In virtually all of these cases, however, there is no prospect of a major act of international aggression comparable to Iraq and Kuwait. The nature of the conflict likely to be fought is much more modest. Moreover, there are no real prospects of a major war in the Middle East because of the capabilities and political circumstances there. The wars between India and Pakistan have tended to be brief border wars and no one thinks there will be a war between the two Koreas except more or less by accident. So that leaves only one possible case of outright aggression: China's attacking Taiwan in an effort to prevent it from becoming independent.

So the historical pattern of (1) great power wars with other great powers, (2) great power wars on smaller countries, and (3) large-scale regional wars—a pattern which has marked international relations for five centuries—really seems to have come to an end.

This has led to a second development which is almost paradoxical. That is that the many people engaged in thinking about international affairs and the conduct of international affairs have started thinking about the constructive use of multilateral military forces, not merely to intervene in cases of genocide, but to go much further and enforce human rights.

This is a total reversal of the view we held before the Cold War, that nation-state borders were inviolable and affairs conducted within borders weren't our business, and that if we didn't abide by that rule, we'd be committing aggression. We believed that each country had to come to certain determinations—the requirements of representative government, the rule of law, and the prohibition of torture—on its own.

Now the elimination of the bipolar world has represented such a dramatic change that people have begun to fault the United Na-

24
.
.
.
.
.

tions and the U.N. regional security system for not being able to successfully conduct major military interventions in regional conflicts, and for not thinking about enforcing human rights.

But all of this is a sign of the extent to which people are ready for that broader kind of thinking. Instead of moving from the end of the Cold War through the next few steps, there was this desire to make a giant leap forward to a totally different world in which we would have some commonly shared standards of behavior that could be enforced by the international community.

A third profound change is the existence of nuclear weapons, which has speeded up thinking about how to get by without war and a belief that we might be able to have a world without war. Even though there are still conservative holdouts who believe that somehow great power wars are going to go on forever and nuclear weapons have nothing to do with it, most people who work in international affairs don't think this.

Another positive trend is that there are many fewer things that people are willing to kill and die for than there were in the past. I see this as a product of a development similar to the declining birth rate. Once you get past a certain level of wealth and well being, you become much more leery of putting your life on the line for things that are outside of your immediate concern. Edward Luttwak, who's very conservative, agrees with me that the tendency to go to war is declining, but he believes the reason for this is that people nowadays only have one or two children so they can't afford to lose them.

Finally, with the changes in South Africa and Russia as well as in other nations, the global spread of democratic institutions has become a foregone conclusion. The sense that there is an increased rate of nationalism and ethnic conflict is wrong. I think that the increase in worrisome trends is much more modest than is widely believed. There have been ethnic conflicts and ethnic wars throughout the twentieth century and with great frequency in many parts of the world. We just didn't pay any attention to them during the nuclear arms race and the Cold War. If you compare the post-Cold War world with the Cold War world, you will find that only in the disintegrating Soviet Union is there a significant change.

All of these changes in the international system and changes in the role of armed force in the international system are very conducive to the viability of the concept of defensive nonviolence as a unifying and bridging concept which will allow us to move towards a substantially different future.

Since I haven't been very successful in promoting defensive non-violence, I've asked myself: If we were *not* to get to a world without war by a path that included government policies moving toward limiting the military to defense, how might we get there otherwise?

What I see is a piecemeal rather than coherent movement to-ward a more peaceful world, a world in which zones of peace or patches of peace are created from the bottom up. I think that there is a possibility that we could have spreading patches of peace being established in different parts of the world in slightly different ways and for slightly different reasons, *all of them* growing together.

The reason that I think it's very important still to focus on de-fensive nonviolence is that I see the possibility that if the world evolves toward peace in a haphazard fasion, the United States could become a kind of warlord in that future peace, and potentially China as well.

The absence of a set of norms embodied in law in the interna-tional system invites that sort of behavior on the part of nation-states. The United States now has nothing keeping it in line. The militarization of U.S. foreign policy during the Cold War—and now after the Cold War—has created a situation in which the United States does not respect the rule of international law.

As things stand now, the United States is going to lead a perma-nent technological arms race which few others can keep up with, let alone engage in. That technological arms race is going to be oriented toward the concept of fighting war with impunity. It will lead to a casual approach toward fighting war. That's an extremely unattractive future. It's not a genuine peace. It's a future in which the bad guys are left to themselves, and we're one of them.

So I would make an appeal to those of you who are committed to no exceptions to the rule of nonviolence to think about taking the toys away from the boys and dismantling the war system, step by step, as an important part of the process of achieving peace.

Response

BY ELISE BOULDING

Randy, you and I have areas of very strong agreement that wars can be brought to an end and that arms limits and reductions are a very useful strategy. I agree strongly with what you said about the critical nature of the next 10 to 20 years. What we do in the next 10 to 20 years will make an enormous difference, not only for the reasons that you lay out but also because of the fact that we're going to have serious water shortages, soil shortages, food shortages, and very likely different kinds of collapses of the global economy.

Certainly, the suicidal nature of the arms race has been well documented since Lewis F. Richardson, going way back to the World War I days. So I agree that we need to buy time through the various proposals that you're putting forth and I agree that the minimum steps *can* be a catalyst.

To rephrase your way of stating the difference in our approaches: It is not the state versus the individual. It's the state versus non-state groupings. I don't think of the culture of peace as being a culture of individuals, although obviously individuals are there.

There are problems that I see. On the one hand, with respect to your statement that certain behavior becomes unthinkable: I like the line of reasoning that says that there are things that become unthinkable over time, but I'm very worried about what has not become unthinkable—cruel torture and cruel punishment have not become unthinkable. In fact, they are increasing. The School of the Americas, of course, is one focus of that, but certainly not the only one.

You are relying on what I would like to be able to rely on more myself: the possibilities of a more peaceable, equitable spread of democracy. However, your last remarks about the U.S. really underscore that the U.S. self-image as a great power is just leading us into all kinds of crazy behavior and creating enemies right and left. The truth is that the U.S. is in decline and doesn't see it. This creates many problems.

As for the cessation of wars of aggrandizement: maybe so, maybe no. I think most of our military activity has been to protect oil supplies and not so much to make things better for people in the places in question. I also think that the high levels of internal violence in the United States make us an unpredictable nation now.

The concept that a basic defensive force—a defensive force is a deterrent force—will always be necessary or likely runs into the historical problem that deterrence doesn't work.

I like your distinction, Randy, between major wars and other wars. There are wars and there are wars. But on the other hand, there's a basic problem that I see as a sociologist looking at history and that is that war socializes people into more aggressive behavior. We're seeing this in the post-Vietnam levels of violence in the U.S. The Great Lakes situation in Africa right now is another very scary example of this and can involve the great powers eventually.

In macro-historical terms, there are periods when there are lots of wars and there are periods when there are fewer wars. But as Sorokin points out, there is no definable trend, just random fluctuations. War weariness cannot be counted on. Otherwise, we wouldn't have war anymore. The number of civilians who have died in wars is enormous. The reasons to be weary of war have always been around.

I would like to shift the focus away from the great powers and the possibility that they're becoming more peaceable to placing more emphasis on small states and the creative leadership that small states can give. Countries like Canada have given leadership to the land mine abolition effort. Civil society movements, of course, have also been a key part of that effort.

Sweden works very much in alliance with NGOs (nongovernmental organizations), as do Norway, the Netherlands, and Costa Rica. These are all countries that are involved, one way or another, in promoting different patterns of state behavior. In my view, states are just not as important as they were, so to put all our eggs in the state basket means ignoring the rise of civil society, of NGOs, and, of course, of the global corporations as well. States are helpless (with respect to many of their policies) in the face of what global corporations choose to do. So I see the need to pay more attention to the civil society and more attention to that part of the civil society which promotes non-offensive defense, civilian-based defense, and the training of citizens to defend their countries without arms.

Seminar #1

The most positive future I can see involves much more interaction among a variety of actors including states, NGOs, intergovernmental organizations, grassroots organizations, and the U.N. system.

Round Table Discussion

"I wonder, Randy," asked Winston Langley, professor of international relations and international law at the University of Massachusetts, "how your proposal would differ from the model that was set up under the United Nations system?" Further, he asked, "May we not run the risk of substituting *defensive* use for *just* war?"

Lending commentary rather than questions to the round table discussion, Paula Gutlove, director of the Program on Promoting Understanding and Cooperation at the Institute for Resource and Security Studies, offered: "I think the goal in the future is to figure out an interactive integration of NGO, government, intergovernmental action, grassroots, and civil society actions. Those I think are the *necessary* not the *conducive* elements to achieving a world without war."

"In order to get to the point where war is unthinkable," she continued, "we have to work on the individual level." Gutlove also suggested that to achieve peace we must learn how to deal with the economics of the arms trade, which is the largest propeller of the U.S. techno-arms race.

"Even if you're only defending," Seyom Brown, Lawrence A. Wien Professor of International Cooperation at Brandeis University, reminded participants, "there's this old saw that you hear with military people that *the best defense is a good offense*. So we must ask, in fact, what constitutes defense?"

Neta Crawford, assistant professor of political science at the University of Massachusetts, offered Dr. Forsberg a semantic distinction: "Perhaps *unthinkable* is not what you mean. *Denormalize* and *delegitimize* are what you are talking about." But, she suggested, there is something more fundamental to be addressed: "Why is it that people use force in the first place?"

In part, she continued, "I think people use force because they believe it is right and effective. They also use force because they have a lack of imagination about alternatives, or the alternatives are weak. Whether or not we can even imagine alternatives or whether the alternatives are institutionally weak is an issue that needs to be beefed up in your conception. I think of two alternatives just off the top of my head. One is sanctions, that is, economic sanctions, political sanctions, sometimes of strategic materials, diplomatic financial sanctions, and the other is robust international institutions, of which we have a few, but we need more."

Saul Mendlovitz, professor of international law at Rutgers University, objected vigorously to the use of the word "nongovernmental." "I'm a member of a citizens' group. I'm a member of civil society," he insisted. "I want a positive statement about the role I'm playing, not a negative one."

Responding to some of the commentary on her presentation, Randy Forsberg offered clarifications: "The idea of sticking to defense would be associated with and could catalyze a culture of peace. It isn't meant to replace a culture of peace."

"If," she continued, "you could get your own country to stick to defense and if all the other citizens could get their countries to do that, together we could actually end war, without taking new risks or bringing about new dangers. I call this a *least change* criterion."

Randy Forsberg referred to the Kuwait/Iraq engagement and said, "At the time when Iraq invaded Kuwait, my feeling was that it was very important for the international community to take action to stop this act of aggression, as a means of showing that the international community will not tolerate the aggressive use of force—that this is not an acceptable standard in the international community. But I found myself virtually alone in what has been called the *peace movement* in the United States. Still, I maintain that if you're going to have the rule of law, you have to set limits and you must enforce them. If you don't, you invite actions like Iraq's invasion of Kuwait."

"Defense against aggression," Dr. Forsberg elaborated, "with military means is acceptable morally and politically and indeed is important as part of the process of ending war. Only when you draw that line very clearly will you be able to establish this norm. Let me reassure you all, however, that under no circumstances do I think that the United States should intervene unilaterally in the Middle East in order to assure the supply of oil at the price that we like, which is, of course, what happened. So it's unfortunate that there was a convergence of distinctly different motives (opposing aggression and protecting access to oil) which were impossible to separate."

"Finally, with respect to people's perception of empowerment: The idea of defensive nonviolence is something that people can relate to. It's part of our everyday experience—from dealing with neighborhood bullies on."

Peace Culture and War Culture: Changing the Balance

BY ELISE BOULDING

This four-part seminar series came out of the discovery that Randy and I were both working on essentially the same task: How to abolish war. We were taking different approaches but they seemed very complementary and challenging.

We're completely united on the goal of the abolition of war. Randy's focus is more on the state actors, the state system, and mine is more on the civil society, the people's organizations, and the extent of peace culture within that civil society. The state and civil society actually interact to create this process that we hope will end war.

I look forward to the kinds of changes that Randy speaks of and writes of that will make war unthinkable—changes that are comparable to the examples of the end of slavery, the end of torture, and the end of cannibalism as normative behavior, and to the likelihood that there may be no major-power wars from now on. But I'm much more pessimistic than Randy is about developing the kinds of skills for peaceful dealing with differences that will make it possible for state decisions to be made that will end war.

The policy-making process of a state reflects the social culture of the society that is making the policies. That means you can't accomplish at a high inter-state level what you don't have any basis for in the habits, attitudes and lifeways of the people.

I think the human race is still in its childhood, frankly. That's an optimistic statement. Something better is possible. The annual reports on torture, child slavery, child prostitution, and other atrocities tell us that these are still very widespread phenomena. We can't, for example, seem to abolish the School of the Americas, which is, among other things, a U.S. torture-training institution. It stays protected by Congress.

I focus on the culture of peace precisely because I see such an overwhelming amount of violence. I have just read Michael Renner's recent Worldwatch pamphlet, *Small Arms, Big Impacts: The Next*

33

Challenge of Disarmament, where he reminds us that between 1989 and 1996, of 101 conflicts, only six were interstate. All the rest are intra-state—254 separate conflict parties. It is clear that the cultures out of which all this fighting comes need help in how they deal with conflict in order to reduce these levels of violence. Eighty percent of the countries that are at war, for example, train children as soldiers. Also, there is a tremendous cross-border flow of arms in every region of conflict.

This has to concern us because war socializes people into violence. Yet, islands of peace emerge and need to be supported. I have recently had a letter from Adam Curle, one of the great Quaker peacemakers of our time. Just back from Bosnia/Croatia, he writes of the peace groups springing up locally out of the overwhelming trauma that people have experienced. They are trying to get back to living normally, to relating to other human beings normally, after the severe physical and emotional traumas they've been through. It is an overwhelming task. Bad as everything is, these little peace groups keep forming—islands of peace culture. They are trying to begin the process of rebuilding the human capacity to care and to relate.

When I talk about "peace culture," I am not talking about a culture that has no conflict in it. Conflict itself is a core fact of social existence, because each of us is different, unique. No two of us are alike. You and I see and experience the world differently, and so does every other human being.

In approaching the concept of peace culture we need to consider two contrasting human needs we all have: one for bonding, to be cared for and to care for others, closeness; the other for autonomy, for our own space.

As individuals, we have to have some human togetherness in our lives, and we have to have space to be who we are as individuals, with all our idiosyncrasies. Getting the right balance between the bonding and the autonomy is what I see as the challenge of peace culture. If everybody just went around bonding and there was no room for individuality, it would be a stifling society, but if everybody went around just fending off everybody else, life would be a constant fight.

In every relationship there is going to be an element of conflict. If we think of conflict management as a continuum, at one end those who are different are simply exterminated. Moving along the continuum we find limited war, threat, and deterrence. In the middle we find arbitration, mediation, negotiation, exchange, mutual adaptation. At the other end of the continuum we find cooperation, integration, and transformation.

Each society can be placed somewhere on this continuum in terms of how it handles the bulk of its conflicts. An individual family can also be placed on that continuum, as can individuals. The issue is not a matter of conflict or no conflict, but of *how we respond to conflict.*

It is very important that so many international and professional associations have signed off on the Seville Statement by UNESCO that war is not biologically inevitable, that it is a social invention. This is essentially a new kind of a statement to make. Our self-image—through history books and the way we teach history in our schools and the way we celebrate it in our public celebrations—is one of making war and winning wars.

The phenomenon of war is a fact of life. The historian William McNeill says that history is essentially the story of power, who wins and who loses. Think of early civilizations and their palace-temple complexes. The temple and the palace were right next to each other and the priests were very much the adjutants of the king or the emperor. It became a religious rite to glorify the wars of the king. The temple was at the heart of the process of the glorification of war, a glorification detailed in the art, the sculpture, the poetry of the time. It all focuses on power: the warrior god demands a holy war; the holy king is a warrior king. Patriarchy means the rule of the strong over the weak, including women and children.

It is important to keep in mind that this religious theme has sanctified war through time by touching a vein of the spirituality of sacrifice and the nobility of sacrifice. This is a distorted spirituality, but one which needs to be recognized.

The religious themes of a culture of peace are very different. Here we find the theme of the loving god, the nurturing god, brotherhood and sisterhood, nonviolence, the holy peace. However, every major religion contains both teachings about a warrior god and a loving, forgiving, reconciling creator. In different forms in different religions, that duality is always present.

In many societies the warrior god and the accompanying template of patriarchy is the more visible theme, while the loving god—the holy peace culture—is never totally absent, but is usually in low key, in the background. Or it may be literally underground and hidden.

Here is my definition of peace culture: *a mosaic of identities, attitudes, values, beliefs, and patterns that lead people to live nurturantly with one another and the Earth itself without the aid of structured power differentials—to deal creatively with their differences and share their resources.* In other words, it includes economic, social, and political structures and processes, and relationships with the environment.

Peace culture is not synonymous with civil society. While civil society certainly represents, in general, a non-military and non force-bound way of solving problems, you can nevertheless have a fairly aggressive civil society. In other words, the autonomy-bonding dichotomy is very much present in the civil society. As a student of nongovernmental organizations (NGOs), I'm very conscious of how many turf battles there are among NGOs as they pursue their different goals and causes. That part of civil society continues to need more civilizing.

There certainly are elements of peace culture in every society, but in some it's much more hidden than in others. It is a tricky thing to try to estimate how much peaceableness there is in everyday life. We do generally negotiate our way through our days, that is, in our families, at school, at work, in various community settings. We tend to negotiate. We don't just fight over every difference. When town meetings break out into fisticuffs, we're shocked. They aren't supposed to do that.

What are the proportions of aggression and negotiation? My late husband Kenneth and I used to argue about this in terms of everyday interactions. He would say that 90 percent of all interaction was peaceful, and I would say we might be lucky if it were 75 percent. Now I think it's less than 75 percent. Bernard Grun's *The Time Tables of History* provides a salutary correction to the overdramatization of war in history books. Studying these pages of parallel activity through the centuries, there is one column for war and state activity, and all the other columns have to do with the whole range of human activities in the arts and the sciences and culture and religion and exploration and adventure. In any period, there is a whole lot going on that doesn't make it into the history books. The Peace Research in History movement provides a corrective in their publications. Also, we are getting some better history writing now.

Where do we look for peace culture? On the one hand, there are elements of peace culture in how we manage our everyday behavioral interactions. On the other hand, we find *islands of peace* in micro-societies, those tribes and indigenous peoples whose lifeways are very peaceful. We find islands of peace among religious groups and communities, such as the historic peace churches, and humanist groups that are committed to nonviolence.

Another form of islands of peace is found in *zones of peace*. This concept goes back to ancient practices of naming holy places, sanctuaries, where people will be safe from attack or punishment. In addition to temples as sanctuaries, over time various diplomatic devices were developed providing safe corridors for movement through the enemy lines. There could also be "temporal" zones of peace. In the Middle Ages, the Catholic Church declared certain days of the week when there would be no fighting. This was known as the Truce of God. Many similar devices for creating times and places of peace and safety in areas of war and violence have developed through the centuries.

Peace culture cannot be discussed without noting the whole issue of the socioeconomic and political structures within which people live. Structural violence is an important concept here, as distinct from behavioral violence. Social, economic, and political structures that distribute the goods and resources and opportunities of a society in such a way that there is severe injustice represent structural violence. When babies die for lack of food, this is structural violence. The peace culture, therefore, must also be thought of in terms of the kinds of socio-economic infrastructures that are present in a society. It must include the strengthening of the peaceful, problem-solving capabilities of a society so that there will be less need for prisons and armies and police.

In addition to creativity in problem-solving, peaceful societies nurture a *utopian longing for peace*. This longing is never totally

37

absent from any society. Warrior societies also cherish legends of warriors putting down their weapons in order to feast, sing, and dance together, in benevolent peaceableness.

Humans have always been able to imagine a state of society different from what they actually experience. If humans could only picture things in their minds based on actual experience, we'd be in a tough spot. But the fact is that throughout history, this utopian imagery of people living in peace never disappears. Utopias are both trenchant critiques of the society that has produced them and signs of the longing for another kind of society.

Fred Polak, the Dutch sociologist whose macrohistorical book I translated in the 1950s on the image of the future, has described how societies are empowered to act in the present by their images of what is possible in the future. If we can visualize viable peace cultures, then that visualization, with suitable attention to the need for analysis, can in fact empower societies to move in the direction of peaceableness.

Let me move on to being more specific on some elements of peace culture. The more I think about it, the more important the issue of child development is. This was reinforced last night in a beautiful talk by Winston Langley, who can't be here today. He spoke about the Declaration of Human Rights, which is approaching its fiftieth anniversary, and the fact that the full development of the human being—growing humans into humans—is the most important thing any society does. But, essentially, this issue is bypassed. We talk about testing, about good curricula, and so on; but the full moral, social, emotional development of the child doesn't get the kind of attention it should. I think what has really happened is that the issue of economic development has swallowed everything else up and so we've lost the sense of what human and social development means.

Bruce Bonta's excellent annotated bibliography of the anthropological literature on peaceful societies, in its summaries of how they function and what makes them peaceful, makes clear to the reader that it is the way that we raise children that determines how grown-ups will handle conflict.

Will the Twa survive? They live in the former Zaire where so much civil war is going on. If I ever go to Africa again, I want to go where the Twa are. For the Twa, the forest is the womb of society, and children are taught to climb trees from a very early age. They spend a lot of time sitting in treetops, looking up into the sky, across through the branches at treetop life, and down below to ground-level life. They look at what the humans are doing, they listen, and they reflect.

If any of you climbed trees as children, you'll relate to this the way I do. Climbing trees is such a special kind of experience because you're rooted to the earth even when you're high up above it. This can generate a very special kind of social and moral development and also a special kind of cognitive development. Children learn how the birds fly and how to recognize different kinds of plants, animals, and insects. The trees are their teachers. When the children fight and have quarrels, this is generally handled by joking and clowning. Parents and others do not get involved in the fight. Adults also use clowning to deal with their quarrels. One good conflict resolution device they use is a tug of war. After the tug of war, everybody falls in a heap so the conflict ends in laughter.

If one grows up with this kind of reflective listening, with constant listening and watching—and clowning—as a part of childhood, as the Twa do, then one is going to be an adult with a lot of resources and a lot of knowledge about how things work in the world.

The Inuit are also a very interesting case because they live in such a marginal, dangerous Arctic environment. The Inuit children are taught to bring home baby animals, to pick up any small creature and to bring it home to be safe and warm and to feed it. There is a lot of cherishing of young animal life. The Inuit have very strong taboos on violent behavior. One does not go around hitting and slapping.

This does not mean that a murder never takes place. In any society there will be pathological behavior. However, the emphasis is on very strong teachings of self-control. A graphic example is given by Jean Briggs, a student of the Inuit. A child will be standing next to his mother who is nursing his baby sister. A relative will call out, "You'd like to kill your baby sister, wouldn't you?" This is very likely what that child was thinking. And then everybody roars with laughter. It's made into a joke. But the thought was real. This kind of teaching, by giving expression to strong negative feelings, and then implying, "Oh well, those kinds of feelings come," and then laughing about them—that is a quite extraordinary thing to be able to do. I would not have had the courage to raise my kids that way, but it creates a society with good skills of self-discipline.

Other examples of teaching children how to handle violent feelings can be found in a variety of peace cultures such as the Anabaptist cultures that go right back to the late Middle Ages. Current versions exist among the Quakers, Mennonites, and Brethren, who all have distinctive ways of teaching children the practices of nonviolence. In Boulder, Colorado, I came to learn how Buddhist families connected with the Naropa Institute teach their children nonviolence. Peace cultures are characterized by a lot of very careful, focused teaching and modeling on how to handle conflict.

While it would be nice to think of the family as the haven of peace culture in every society, we also know that there is a great deal of violence in families. The patriarchal template has authorized the use of force and the beating of women and children. That makes it tricky to talk about and work with the concept of the family as the place where children and adults learn and practice peaceful ways. It obviously is a key setting for such learning, but it can never be taken for granted that that is what is going on. We need community input that models peaceful parenting and peaceful spousal relations and that gives children opportunities to learn how to deal with differences nonviolently.

However, there's a willful blindness, I think, on the part of many people in various peace communities. They don't want to know how much violence goes on in families. I've made a very great effort to overcome my own blindness to that and to accept the fact that we can never take it for granted that the family will be a center of peace and love. However, when there is a community culture that supports peaceful behaviors, a child growing up in that environment has a good head start on being a peacemaker and a problem-solver. Problem-solving is basic to the concept of peace culture. The peacemaker way of life isn't just a state of bliss, but a way of living in the world that deals with all of the conflicts and the differences that are part of daily life.

One thing that I have come to see as more and more important myself as the years go by is the importance of play. Because we had five children and they're all two years apart, I spent a big chunk of my life with children, and our home was always filled with neighborhood children. I came to value what play was—and the kind of imagination and problem-solving behavior and skills that children learn as they play. It's fantastic.

One year I did a study of play life in families. Some volunteer families kept journals which recorded individual activities of each family member, including play activity. I discovered that children play *for* their parents. In effect, they entertain their parents. It's as if the parents are just loving the fact that they can sit and watch their kids play. But the adults often don't know how to play themselves. A family where everybody gets in and plays together is not very common. Adults have a very underdeveloped play life. To recover an ability to play is very important for a peace culture. We need civic celebrations in peaceful societies—celebrations where there's a lot of singing and dancing and fun. We have a certain amount of fun on the Fourth of July, for example, but the firecrackers remind us that we are celebrating a war that we won. Reflecting on the role of celebrations that release the playfulness in us (which is part of our creativity) also helps us with our intellectual playfulness—the play of the imagination, the play of the mind. We've gotten terribly stiff in this respect.

In concluding today, I will return to the theme of zones of peace as islands of peace culture, and save for my next lecture a discussion of various strategies for getting from our present war-prone world to a more peaceful one.

An important beginning step toward more complete zones of peace in recent decades has been the creation of a number of nuclear weapon-free zones by states in various regions. The first such zone was created by the Treaty of the Antarctic, to be followed by the Treaty of Tlatelolco in Latin America, the Treaty of Raratonga in the Asia-Pacific, the Treaty of Bangkok in South Asia, and the Treaty of Pelindaba in Africa. In addition, the treaties on outer space and the seabed also include a commitment to keeping these spaces nuclear-free, but these are honored more in the breach than the observance. The significance of these treaties lies in the widespread creation of a nuclear-free norm, and efforts continue for such treaties in North America and Europe, where resistance on the part of major powers is strong. Each treaty specifically declares an intention to move toward a future general and complete disarmament. NGOs played an important role in the creation of each treaty and offer hope for ongoing collaboration between NGOs and governments for the goal of a disarmed world.

The zone of peace concept permits many gradations from a nuclear-free zone to a culture of peace. The latter has captured the imagination of various civic groups around the world with the result that a number of towns have declared themselves zones of peace. This has led to the development of community mediation services, peer mediation programs in schools, the establishment of sister-city relationships on other continents, and a re-examination of the economic, social, and political life of the town. This approach moves from theoretical discussions about peace to practical local actions, and holds promise for the future.

I have indicated some ways in which peace culture is present in our world, although socially invisible. The resources are there for it to expand. The reason I am working on a book on this subject is to call attention to current social movements within civil society that will make peace cultures more visible as they bring new skills and new ideas of alternative ways to solve problems into the public arena. There are promising developments. It is the interaction of the peace culture elements of civil society with the state system, whose potentials Randy has so well analyzed, that will make a peaceful world. I see the approaches that Randy and I espouse as intimately interconnected.

Response

BY RANDALL FORSBERG

I'm going to group my comments into three parts. One is to focus on a part of what Elise said that I particularly liked. The second is to talk a little bit about the contrast between her approach and my approach. And then, third, I'm going to go back to what she said today and just make a few observations.

The thing that I particularly liked was that Elise added on to her printed definition of peace culture *(the mosaic of identities, attitudes, values, beliefs, behaviors in which people treat each other and the Earth nurturantly)* the phrase: *without the aid of a structured power differential.* I think that's a really intriguing, interesting, attractive image of the future.

What it conjures up in my mind is something that I'm going to come back to in my *ad hoc* remarks: the difference between small, simple societies and large, complex societies or civilizations or nation-states. One of the important differences, historically, that relates to social endorsement of violence has been the existence of a pyramid of power in the complex societies which contrasts with the more egalitarian and participatory nature of simple societies.

The idea (or one of the ideas) behind the development of contemporary modern democratic values and culture has been to try to flatten the pyramid of power and to create exactly this relationship of people being able to interact creatively and peacefully, not because the extent of power and application of power is different and well-defined, but because of a different and well-defined set of guidelines or limits that can't be crossed, and rather out of an internalized respect for the other person—an ability, as Elise has been emphasizing, to deal with differences and problems and conflicts creatively and imaginatively, and to grow and be transformed by them rather than letting them define your relationship.

I think that that definition of a peace culture which Elise gave in the middle of her talk is really a very useful synthesis and capsule of what a world without war might be like—or a world without socially-sanctioned violence.

43
.
.
.
.
.

Let me turn now to the differences in our two approaches, which is going to be (as it should be and will be) a theme of all of the four presentations. Elise began by saying that of course the behavior of the state mirrors the state of the culture. I certainly agree with that and in no way assume the state can be expected to perform in a manner that is not consistent with the values that are prevalent in the culture or that the state can somehow reshape (or have the capacity to reshape) the values of the culture.

I would like to comment on the uncomfortable relationship between these two approaches and to propose another way of looking at it. In focusing on the state, I distinguished between approaches oriented to the state government policy and approaches oriented to individual behavior, and this caused some controversy on the grounds that this wasn't the appropriate contrast. It should be the state versus the civil society and, in particular, nongovernmental organizations.

As I thought that over afterwards, I felt that there had certainly been some misunderstanding. This relates to how I see the state and culture interacting. I think what I had been intending to convey was that an important difference between those two approaches is that which concerns what the nongovernmental organizations are attempting to accomplish.

What I was trying to suggest was that if nongovernmental organizations were to focus on certain goals for changes in state policy, that could help structure a larger political and cultural transformation. I saw that type of approach as being contrasted with nongovernmental organizations focusing on the transformation of individual behavior, family behavior, and community behavior.

In both cases, in my case as well as Elise's, the objective is to define a useful agenda for the associations in civil society to work toward a world without war. And the point I had been trying to make was that there's a very big difference between nongovernmental organizations focusing on what would bring about a change of a certain kind in government policy—on the one hand, government policy relating to war and peace, national government policy—and nongovernmental organizations focusing on what would bring about changes in individual behavior and community behavior of a kind which would, in turn, foster government policy change.

Keeping that in mind, I would like to amend what I said in our first session by commenting that my interest in having nongovernmental organizations focus on government policy change is largely because I think it's the most effective way to bring energy to bear for the kinds of cultural changes that Elise is talking about. I absolutely do not think that government policy can change otherwise, so it's a tactical difference.

Finally, some comments not on our differences but on our common interests. I want to make three or four statements that relate to the idea of violence as it impinges on the idea of peace. The first is that I think I have an optimistic view of the potential for peace that exists in daily life. That view is rooted in the idea, among other things, that when children are socialized, they basically learn just a few main rules, like controlling your bodily functions and not hitting other people, and maybe something to do with deferred gratification—a relationship between means and ends.

Those are the fundamental components of the socialization process that goes on between about two months and ten years. This is a sort of internal limit setting. I think that this happens in every culture, regardless of whether it's simple or complex. Every child learns, for example, that it's not okay to bite and kick and hit and scratch—among other things.

I would say that part of being a socialized adult is first learning that you can't do these things and then, on top of that learning, discovering that there are certain exceptional situations in which you can or you're expected to or it's widely done or you'll be praised for doing the opposite of what you've been taught.

The foundation for a culture of peace is broader, more fundamental, and more widely shared than I think Elise suggested. And in relation to that, let me make just one other main point about violence and peace. It is helpful to distinguish between the absence of war (or the absence of violence), on the one hand, and the presence of an egalitarian and nurturing society on the other hand. But it is not helpful to equate structural violence with war. The reason has to do with what I just said about children. There's a "first-do-no-harm" rule. People need to learn not to use violence at any level. This is a very basic and very simple idea. It doesn't solve a lot of problems, but it permits problem-solving.

The idea that we can create a genuinely egalitarian participatory society that meets human needs is a concept that goes far beyond the absence of war. To say that what we need to do in establishing peace is to create this terrific society without structural violence is, I think, inadequate.

Peace, in the sense of nonviolence, is a very limited goal. It's not utopian at all. And I think that it can be achieved and that we should make it a goal to have limits on violent behavior recognized as appropriate in adult communities in the same way that, individually, children learn this rule. We should not let people believe that, unfortunately, this nonviolent state can not be arrived at until everybody has a good life. I just don't think that's true. I think that that is a stunning example of this upside down way of looking at things.

I just received and read some literature on a new action called the Hague Peace Appeal, which has been initiated by the International Physicians for the Prevention of Nuclear War, the International Alliance of Lawyers Against Nuclear Arms, the International Peace Bureau, and Peace Action. They talk about the agenda for a meeting in the Hague in 1999 that will commemorate the 100th anniversary of the Hague Peace Conference. One of the things on the agenda is looking at the root causes of war. And then the agenda also includes topics like poverty. Not mentioned in those root causes, or in most of the discussions of this kind, is empire building by wealthy nations who have more resources and more access to military power. The causes of war are described as though war primarily came from the poor and the disenfranchised.

In my view, certainly the large wars, the big devastating huge wars, are just the opposite. They are imposed on the already disenfranchised by the powerful.

Round Table Discussion

"The issue of peace and justice is the one I'd like to see addressed," Neta Crawford, assistant professor of political science at the University of Massachusetts began. "Richard Goldstone, who was the head of the War Crimes Tribunals for Rwanda and Yugoslavia until recently, argued that the reason conflicts recur in places like Rwanda and Yugoslavia is that justice never took place in the last war. Does the imposition of war crimes tribunals actually help deter and reconcile people or does it do something much worse, which is to label the criminal as different and outside? I'm wondering if amnesties and reparations are better and lead to a peaceful culture?"

"I want to raise some questions about the nature of community," Michael True, convener of the Nonviolence Commission of the International Peace Research Association, began. "How are we going to create a peace community? It seems to me that substantial social change occurs only when a lot of people are willing to go to jail for it. What are the initiatives that are going to bring about the necessary psychological changes so that people can be brave and courageous and yet not kill people?"

"I'm very excited by this discussion," Barbara Hildt, project director of the North Essex Prevention Coalition, told the co-convenors. "I see the importance of what both of you are talking about, working with NGOs on a political level to change public policy and also creating islands of peace."

"Cultures are not static," John Montgomery, Ford Foundation Professor of International Studies Emeritus at Harvard University, reminded participants, "so the issue is: How can we move cultures toward peace? Related to this: How do we deal with assumptions that are unwholesome? What sorts of things can we do to give people access to their rights?"

Addressing what he called the issue of *maximized pluralism,* Dr. Montgomery continued: "It seems to me that the more you understand and appreciate other people, the less likely you are to see them as villains. We can all be peacemakers. I think it's very important not to set down one side—such as women—as the people who work for peace and exclude everybody else."

As his final observation, Dr. Montgomery approached the subject of policy: "Policies are made by people who have the power to make policies, and policies can be influenced by people." He urged that we all remember that there are "all kinds of people who can do all kinds of things to make peace possible."

"If one embraces your philosophy and prescriptions for building the peace culture, Elise," Seyom Brown, Lawrence A. Wien Professor of International Cooperation at Brandeis University, added, "we're left with the question of the phasing out of the alternative culture: what we keep, what we dispense with, and how quickly, along the way toward a fuller realization of the peace culture. We need to include these matters in our discussion."

"Peacekeeping was conceived by Sir Brian Urquhart to mean lightly armed mediators trained to use their arms only in self defense," Virginia Mary Swain, co-director of Cambridge-based The Center for Global Community and World Law, observed. "It's a great concern to me that military troops are assigned peacekeeping posts without mediation training. Disastrous and well-documented results have demonstrated the carnage from untrained soldiers using firearms without this understanding."

"We must find alternatives that will enable people to interface without constructing hierarchies and pyramids of power," Loyal Rue, professor of religion and philosophy at Luther College, suggested. "I think it's very important to work at the very early levels of human nurturance so that the hierarchy-seeking impulses don't get socialized."

Responding to some of the observations shared, Elise Boulding took up the question of the War Crimes Tribunals. "They create," she indicated, "the whole punishment syndrome—the opposite of reconciliation. I've heard so many stories of victims who feel totally abandoned because there hasn't been enough acknowledgment of their suffering. The truth has been told but nobody has said, 'I'm sorry,' in a way that means something to the victims. You've got a residue of emotional bitterness there. I think we have to acknowledge that we have not yet discovered a good mechanism for truth-telling as a basis for reconciliation."

"I find heartening," Randy Forsberg added, "that mediation as an alternative to violence and as a mechanism for building up a sense of community seems to be growing by leaps and bounds in this country."

"With respect to policy and culture," she continued, "I would add that the interaction between policy, culture, and nationalism or ethnocentrism is also an important variable to consider. Just look at the current Israeli administration and contrast it with the last to see an example of how government can inflame or soothe."

Adding his own insight, John Montgomery enlarged the topic: "Within the cycle when nationalism is on the rise and you have the greatest risk of warlike language, you also have the greatest opportunity for peacemakers to intervene. You not only have cycles, but you also have counter-cycles. The real task of the peacemaker is to identify the opportunities of counter-cyclical behavior."

Addressing Seyom Brown's inquiry, Randy Forsberg provided some clarifying remarks: "What I have stressed is the confusion in people's minds between using violence to defend oneself when one is violently attacked and accepting war as an inevitable feature of human culture. People have to understand that to reserve the right to defend yourself if you are attacked is not the same as to accept the perpetuation of war and war culture."

"The fact that there is a police system," she continued, "and that parents can pull fighting children apart and that people may need to be protected from bullies does not mean that we live in a culture that allows, condones, or promotes violence."

"I'd like to raise the issues of patriotism and of the media and the lopsided views conveyed to school children," Karen Nardella, program manager at the Boston Research Center, interjected.

Picking up on these themes, Elise responded: "You take me right back to the forties and fifties when our kids were being urged to buy war bonds at school. They were getting one view of the world at school and a totally different view at home. The school system doesn't really critique the media. We have to work on the complicity of the schools and the media in giving children a skewed presentation of the world."

"With respect to the problem of gender," Carol Cohn, who teaches sociology and women's studies at Bowdoin College, offered, "so many of the things you've talked about are not valued—such as peacemaking—precisely because they're associated with the feminine. As the culture stands now, despite the real gains of the women's movement, the feminine is still valued much less than the mascu-

49

line. I think that anything that continues to be marked as *feminine* can never become a cultural priority. This is an impediment to some of the things that you're envisioning."

Concluding, author Robert A. Irwin challenged both Randy and Elise for "being too eager to agree with each other on the point that one can't get more out of the state than the culture allows."

"There's certainly," he observed, "very solid common sense in that. But the creative opportunities are precisely where that generalization is invalid. The state is not a unitary element. It's a lot of conflicting elements."

Process of Demilitarization: Unilateral and Multilateral Steps

BY RANDALL FORSBERG

Today I am going to discuss government action to move us closer to a world largely without war—a world in which acts of war are rare, small in scale, and quickly ended.

At our previous session, we discussed focusing not on government policy, nor on individual behavior and norms, but on nongovernmental organizations (NGOs) as vehicles for change, or the locus of change, in matters of war and peace. Earlier, there was a good deal of confusion when I made a distinction between governmental change and individual change. Elise and others responded, "Yes, but what we're talking about is not individual change; it's action on the part of nongovernmental organizations, grassroots organizations, civic associations." I want to underscore the fact that I, too, am thinking about activities on the part of such organizations. The question is: What is the audience for their campaigns? What is the objective? What is the information and motive to action which they attempt to convey to a larger group of individuals who are not yet involved but whom they want to mobilize and make involved? Are they attempting to generate change in the lives and behavior of individuals, or in government policy?

In the case of my approach, the changes in government policy that I propose are put forward in the hope that nongovernmental organizations will include a demand for such changes in their activities. I would ask, then: If civic organizations are working effectively to create a world without war, what are the goals of those organizations for change in government policy and in intergovernmental institutions, norms, and practices? I'm going to suggest certain goals as meriting the highest priority in the policy-change agenda of NGOs.

In brief, the concept, which I introduced at the first session, is the creation of a defensively-oriented global security system in which shared norms and practices cut across various countries. The system is characterized by two main features: first, *the use of armed*

51

force or violence for any purpose except defense is explicitly and fully renounced; and second, *countries agree to come to each other's aid if any one of them is attacked by a country or a faction which doesn't accept this norm of defensiveness.* So the global security system is collective and it is defensively-oriented.

The idea of limiting the military to defense is not new. The more I look, the more references I find to this concept, including one which Bob Irwin kindly pointed out in Elise's book, *The Underside of History.* The reference there is to a woman [Christine de Pisan] who lived in the thirteenth century who had a really fine plan for a defensively-oriented collective security system. There are also references to defensive security in Greek literature and in Confucian literature. In sum, there is a very long history to the idea that if people just limited any use of armed force to defense, then no one would be attacked and there would not be any war.

Similarly, the idea of a system of governance in which people collectively as well as individually agree to come to each other's aid if attacked is not new. In essence, it means saying that any of us may be too weak, on our own, to defend ourselves; but if we all agree to defend each other, then surely as a group we would be strong enough to withstand the predations of bullies and rogues and imperialists and exploiters and so on. One early version of this idea was proposed by Dante Alighieri in 1312.

What then is the reason to raise these ideas now? Apart from the fact that they seem to be of a piece with many other values and practices involved in the global spread of democracy, apart from the fact that they seem right, *for the first time* developments in world politics are profoundly conducive to the possibility of both establishing such a defensively-oriented collective security system and having it succeed in preventing war.

Specifically, there are three developments which are conducive to the success of a defensive security system as a means of ending war, two of which have been going on throughout the twentieth century and the third since the end of the Cold War.

The first is the spread of belief in self-determination, a core democratic idea. This has been demonstrated most powerfully in the abolition of colonialism and the falling into disrepute of the great power behavior which still characterized British and French policy into the 1960s or Portugal (in Angola) in the 1970s. Beginning with India's agitation in the early decades of the century, the colonial empires persisted throughout the post-World War II era in processes of disintegration and reversion of political control to the indigenous populations.

In addition to the end of colonialism, there are many areas where dictatorships of one sort or another have been gradually transformed by more democratic practices. These changes all reflect the moral concept that individuals don't have the right to use violence to persuade each other to accept certain political or economic or social arrangements. Another way of putting this is that respect for the dignity of the individual requires that political decision-making should involve laws, practices, and procedures, but not violence.

In sum, in the twentieth century the global tendency in national organization is toward more self-determination, greater democracy, greater respect for the dignity and worth of the individual, and the inviolability of the individual within the polity. That trend has roots which go back several centuries, among other things, to the founding of the United States; but it is most marked in the twentieth century.

Secondly, the development of television and radio and film and airplanes has brought the world closer together. Today individuals in all parts of the world literally can see individuals in other parts of the world on the news—or in films—and see how they live, what their lifestyles and their cultures are like. This has made it much more difficult to maintain what has been a long-standing, widespread human experience: recognizing the dignity and worth of individuals internally in one's own culture but not in other cultures.

In many simple cultures the word for human being means "the person who is a member of this culture," while other humans out there are animals or not fully human beings. The same tendency to distinguish—but in a less drastic way—has been true among complex nations and cultures where people were disqualified from the standards and norms that one applies to one's own kind because of their ethnic, racial, linguistic, or religious background. Though still troublingly present in today's world, the barriers of strangeness and unfamiliarity have been falling, and tolerance has been growing.

Finally, the end of the Cold War has removed a structural contribution to the perpetuation of militarism and nationalistic military policies, a problem which is referred to by political scientists as the "security dilemma." The concept is that two equally powerful nations, even if committed not to use force except for self defense, may still engage in a qualitative arms race or a quantitative arms build-up. They may even undertake preemptive attacks—defensively-oriented but preemptive—because frequently in war offensive measures can strengthen defense.

As long as each of two nations perceives increases in the security—defined as the war-winning capability—of the other as decreases in its own security, the two will be locked in the security dilemma, that is, the dilemma that what's protective for one is damaging or threatening to the other. The arms race between the United States and the former Soviet Union had a lot of that character, with both sides claiming to be defensive and yet acquiring offensive weapons and build-ups and new technology in order to be assured of being able to defend themselves. Today, in contrast, there is no longer a sense of a direct and opposite impact of military choices by any two large countries.

So, if we look at the first two factors—the tendency toward self-rule and, more broadly, democracy and the shrinking globe—we can say that broader trends have been moving in a direction conducive to the abolition of war and the establishment of a defensively-oriented collective security system. The end of the Cold War contributed or added to those broader trends, removing the obstacle to such a system of this traditional approach to security which involved two parties that caught the whole world up in their confrontation, not just two nearby countries.

Having a unipolar world means that we can side-step the argument that a given nation has to be stronger not because it has aggressive plans but in order to defend itself against a potential opponent who's doing the same thing. Views of this kind no longer obstruct the establishment of a much more defensively-oriented security system.

Because of all of these changes, the United States and the European countries and Russia are already taking some steps that can be characterized as a defensively-oriented security system. In particular, I'm thinking about the greatly increased importance that the United States has put on consulting with allies and building a consensus for military action. In Iraq, we have tried for consensus as contrasted with, let's say, what the United States did 20 or 30 years ago in Vietnam, or Central America, where the idea that you needed to have an international consensus—that a given action was in fact defensively-oriented—before you could take action was never introduced.

(Actually, it's wrong to say it never appeared on the horizon in the U.S. because Adlai Stevenson certainly tried to get the U.N. behind various moves of the United States, and there was always some talk of international law and international legitimacy but that was intended to be much more *pro forma* than it is today.)

The idea is gaining support that for the U.S. to unilaterally dictate what will happen in Iraq may be counterproductive; that the way to deal with Iraq is to have the authority of the international community and the support of international law, with its moral authority. I think that lesson about unilateralism has begun to be taken by U.S. government officials and the government bureaucracy. So I'm very encouraged by that, even though it's an early step and it's still in a kind of attenuated form compared with what we'd like to see.

Civil Society's Response

There are encouraging trends. What is missing is a deliberate effort on the part of nongovernmental organizations to encourage government policies to promote peace, or on the part of governments to develop such policies. There is no deliberate effort to create a global security system which will work very much in the manner that the U.N. was originally intended to work—a system in which countries have renounced the use of force except for defense, where the strong agree to come to the aid of the weak in case that's needed, and there is no war.

In spite of the propitious developments, there's no effort to take advantage of this special time. There's no rushing into the vacuum and saying, "We can accomplish now what people have thought about and talked about for such a long time."

The question I want to address now is: If there were such a campaign, what would be its main elements, and by what kind of process might it move forward?

The principal elements of a campaign of this kind would be, first of all, *to establish the preeminence of the rule of law* and, in particular, the non-use of force as an instrument of policy in international relations. The thing that is most troubling about the unilateral power of the United States in trying to prevent Iraq from getting weapons of mass destruction—or using force to end an act of international aggression or an act of genocide—the thing that's a problem with one country doing this, is that it suggests that the way to behave in the international arena is *ad hoc*,"to each according to his (military) abilities": If you can and you're so disposed, fine, and if not, that's fine too. If the strong want to do something that's good for everybody, that's great; if they don't, if they want to be empire-builders, well, that's very sad, but that's just how the chips fall.

There's no sense of an international legal and political milieu in which there are shared standards of what to expect and what to work for and how countries ought to behave. It undermines standards for one country to arrogate the power to itself, to decide if and when to use armed force to support what are generally accepted moral or legal norms.

What I mean by establishing the *preeminence of the rule of law* is that the common norms in the international system should supersede the powers of individual nations to act or not to act in given situations. More specifically, what that would mean is that we need to have multinational or multilateral rather than unilateral decision-making and action, if such action is needed to respond to threats to peace such as the development of weapons of mass destruction or breaches of peace like genocide or cross-border aggression.

We not only need to have practices and policies for multilateral action, but we also need, specifically and explicitly, for nations to renounce unilateral action to protect national interests outside of national territory.

There aren't many places where you can look at national policy statements and say, "See, this is wrong; this is right," because people tend to use euphemisms that co-opt the debate. But one of the few places where you *can* look and find something that is an overt expression of a bad principle which directly undermines the development of a global peace system is the statements on the part of the

United States—and some other countries—that they are prepared to use force *to protect national interests anywhere in the world.*

That is not a law-abiding kind of a statement. If you translate it or you look at the analogy to that statement in domestic affairs, if you had an individual citizen saying, "I'm prepared to use force to protect my interests," that is not a defensive use of force. It's not a moral or a legal use of force either within nations or between nations.

As long as the United States includes in its national policy statements that it is maintaining military capabilities to protect national interests around the world—or reserving the right to use military force to protect national interests around the world—then the United States is not supporting the principle that individual nations don't have the right to use force for anything except to defend themselves if other people are attacking them or defend neighbors if other people are attacking them. It's not committing itself to defensive uses of armed force and to the rule of law. The rule of law must be preeminent.

Secondly, there could be vastly strengthened means of nonmilitary conflict resolution which are institutionalized, developed, supported, funded, studied, taught, and practiced in order that the international community not be put in the position of stressing fighting wars as the primary means of ending wars. The international community needs to develop the strongest possible nonmilitary means of resolving or defusing conflicts before they turn into wars.

Finally, on the military side there needs to be a process by which reliance on national armed force for defense and for defense of oneself, defense of other nations, or to be used in humanitarian ways—reliance on national forces—is replaced by reliance on multinational forces where the very important point is not so much who does the killing and dying, although that is important, but who decides what killing and dying is going to be done.

As long as you have one country providing the majority of the troops for any military action, then that country is likely to be making the decision about when nonmilitary means have been exhausted and when it's time to use force and when the balance of suffering is such that these risks and deaths should be accepted rather than those, as we all saw in the case of the Gulf War.

Those three goals may not be a complete list of what would need to be done in order to create a global security system that would be likely to have the effect of making war very rare, but they represent a strong beginning.

Potential Problems

Generally speaking, there are two kinds of problems that people have with proposals of this kind. The first one is the idea that you can't end war by fighting wars; you can't create a multilateral law enforcement system which relies on armed force as a central component of the process to end war. People believe you have to rely exclusively on nonmilitary means—and such means exist and would provide a morally and politically consistent position and are much more likely to be successful in achieving the goal.

Essentially, opponents of these concepts argue, the idea of relying on military means is a slippery slope and involves a lot of ambiguities and contradictions, morally and politically. The concept, they say, is just not likely to work. It's more likely to be subverted than to be effective. I talked about this point in my first presentation.

The second objection, which I am going to respond to today, is that while the concept of government policies aimed at moving toward a world without war is a nice idea—and a lot of people, except for the first group, could agree with it (and you might expect the majority of the public in the United States and most other countries to think that this was a good thing)—in practice it's not likely to be workable because the sources of resistance are just far too great.

With respect to this and other objections, there are, in fact, ways of creating a transitional regime which is likely to raise fewer obstacles than just proposing to jump from here to there wholesale. There are ways for nations to try out what it would be like to restrict national sovereignty to the extent required for a system of this kind to work, to try it out without committing ourselves to it permanently and irrevocably. It is not wise to give people an all-or-nothing choice, one in which you either establish a world government of which people are fearful and suspicious and which they think can't be trusted to do the right thing and might exploit its power, or else you have unchecked, unilateral national military power. You provide some kind of middle ground which is, in this case, a *transitional regime.*

The idea of the transitional regime that I recommend is that we can practice sharing power while we still maintain our own unilateral military power or our legal right to use power unilaterally. We can enter into an agreement to practice multilateral intervention for 10 years; we can make a tentative commitment not to undertake unilateral intervention as long as everything is going smoothly.

The idea of this is where the commitment is easily reversible, there is reason to believe that just entering into this kind of agreement would lower pressures and reduce incidents. The new behavior would put pressure on the effort to work multilaterally. It would be establishing norms and changing expectations in the international arena. There would be an entirely new feeling about legitimate uses of force that would be spread by this trial component.

The obstacles are very high, as is the skepticism on the part of individuals, but this is really going to end up being a route we will be glad we have taken. The objection that we can't know in advance if a security system we've never tried is going to work the way we wish it would is a strong objection. We need to deal with that objection by practicing non-intrusive, non-coercive protection.

As a process response to this idea that the obstacles to a collective security system are too high, I want to draw your attention to what are currently the objectives—or the focus—of NGO campaigns which are aimed at changing government policy.

With very few exceptions, insofar as NGO groups are focusing on government policy rather than on education or community or individual behavior, they tend to fall toward what I would argumentatively call one of two extremes. The one extreme is *very* incremental change at the margin: "Don't build the F-22," or "Don't build the MX," or "Cut military spending by 5 percent."

The extreme of incremental change involves a very small, very focused, chipping away kind of approach. I have to say that I would even put the issue of banning landmines in there. It's as if we ask, "If we can ban chemical weapons, biological weapons, landmines, and we can get nuclear weapons cut back—if we can we get governments to stop doing as many bad things as possible—won't this eventually undermine the war system?"

The other extreme is an effort to effect wholesale change in government policies worldwide with respect to matters of war and peace. For example, "Abolish nuclear weapons." The role of nuclear weapons is to deter conventional war. Conventional war is still a very big problem. We're raising the question about whether it isn't too big to really try to do anything substantial and organized to stop it. I suggest that there's no way that nuclear weapons are going to be abolished while the conventional war system is in place.

So the NGO campaign to abolish nuclear weapons is at the other extreme pole from the individual weapons system campaign. It's as if there are only two choices: Change something that's *very* incremental or change something that's *very* massive.

Other examples of NGO-sponsored kinds of tactics are efforts to establish a world government and campaigns for general and complete disarmament. There is also the campaign to bring about universal conscientious objection to war. These are the kinds of universal global change I would call good with respect to the war problem, but also massive. There's no bridge. There are no intermediate stepping stones.

It's not appropriate for NGOs to take only these two extreme positions. We need to develop a demand to place on governments which is in the center, in the sense of requiring sufficiently large steps that we know that, if they're taken, they're going to lead to a very different world.

NGOs need to have a campaign for incremental but fundamental global change. It's fine for NGOs to do all the other things—to have anti-individual weapons system campaigns and conscientious objector campaigns and nuclear abolition campaigns. What's not fine is *not* to have a campaign for a defensive global security system which could conceivably be implemented if enough people thought it was a good idea. There isn't any other obstacle to this than the usual consciousness-raising obstacle for all social change efforts. In my judgment, it's abandoning responsibility, it's abandoning the peace process, not to have a campaign of this kind.

Response

BY ELISE BOULDING

I agree very much with the last point you made, Randy, about the need for NGOs to work for both incremental and fundamental global change.

We have different degrees of optimism which have emerged in both the previous sessions on the extent to which things are going "our" way. You've made the point very well that the talk about moving to defensive warfare, as long as it's not couched in national interest language, makes sense.

But something important happened in Europe—the 1987 treaty for weapons reduction—which is hardly celebrated at all, but has been effective. The European NGOs were very much involved, as was International Peace Research Association (IPRA), in helping to bring this about. So literally, lowering overall arms levels *has* happened in Europe, although, unfortunately, in the rest of the world it has not.

Also, while it's true that there is a new sense of a global community because of TV, I'm afraid that the dangers of a *glib globalism*, of thinking we understand more than we do understand, has taken over—especially with the American public. Intercultural interaction is an extremely tricky, sensitive, complex thing. To think that because we watch people in the rain forest or in battle in Somalia we really understand what is going on, that is cause for alarm. NGOs have a responsibility to work on understanding the complexity of world events—and particularly to understand and interpret the anti-West backlash.

Almost every day now I read more about how much damage the West is doing to the world. The issue isn't just Asian values versus Western values, although that sometimes comes up. It's more an issue of what has modernization and what has industrialization done to the non-Western world?

In the West we approach thinking of one world and the welfare of the world with two strikes against us in the sense that we do not represent world interest in the way that we would like to think we do.

61

In your writings, Randy, you have mentioned the U.S. downsizing and going from a two-war to a one-war strategy. I thought we were on a three-war strategy now and that we were going from a three-war to a two-war strategy. We still have a ways to go. I'd like you to comment on this. Also, why do we insist on keeping our nukes on hairline trigger alert? Why are we so unwilling to set any timetable for nuclear disarmament for ourselves? We seem to have the attitude that, "It's okay for everybody else but not for us." This extreme resistance and the outrageous allocation of funds to new high-tech breakthroughs and a new generation of weapons—this is all terribly dangerous.

The usual economic arguments about the defense industry were exploded years ago—back in the fifties and the sixties. It has now been shown that military industries are very bad for national economies. It makes no sense that the U.S. is still stuck in this view that we've got to keep our factories going and we've got to keep our weapons labs going for the sake of the economy.

A gradual decrease of weapons is, by all means, necessary. Here I would like to point out that I see a good process going on right now and that's the nuclear weapon-free zones that I mentioned in my last presentation. These are national policies undertaken at a regional level. They're relevant for national defense policy.

There's a splendid new book just out from the U.N. Institute for Disarmament Research, *Nuclear Weapon-Free Zones in the 21st Century*. I recommend it to all of you as an example of the interaction of people's associations and states and the U.N., a three-way interaction.

Each of the nuclear weapons-free zone treaties has a clear statement that this is *the first step to further disarmament*. That's very, very important. That's exactly the kind of incrementalism that we're talking about. NGOs can provide a lot of social leadership for moving faster in this area. But these treaties also make room for the nervous security-conscious government officials who want to keep as much of the status quo as possible. So there is a play in the system, which is important.

Creative people with creative social imaginations have been doing a great deal, especially in Latin America. And people's associations have been responsible for a lot of the successes. People like

Juan Somavia, with experience in the NGO world and also in government and in the U.N., have been key figures in the whole weapons-free zone process.

There are about 24 states that have declared themselves to be non-nuclear and unwilling to maintain military defenses. They are the seedbeds for nuclear weapons-free regions. We also have the fascinating example of Mongolia standing up and saying, okay, we're a nuclear-free zone. They're in one of the world's hot spots and yet they are going around giving talks about the importance of individual states setting examples. So there's a lot happening which isn't getting much attention.

Agreements on cutting down the arms trade seem to be very difficult to achieve except in the context of these kinds of agreements where all the states in a region act in concert. So regionalism is very important in getting to disarmament. Let me point out that the U.S., the U.K., and France have been dragged kicking and screaming to these treaties. Some of the treaties they have not signed, others they have. But if they don't guarantee upholding the treaties, of course that's a problem. So we really have to work on getting the big powers to follow the example of the lesser powers.

I like your point that we're setting new norms, and norms develop over time. But I would remind us that the concept of a world in which national defense is purely defensive, and war-making equipment is not maintained, really goes back to 1899 and the Hague Peace Conference. That was the first time that we had an international statement of a new behavioral norm. So here we are, one hundred years later, getting ready to hold the hundredth anniversary meeting of the Hague Peace Conference, and maybe we're a little further along. But let's not think we've moved very fast. It's taken one hundred years to accept these norms, at least at a verbal level. They are certainly not accepted at the behavioral level.

It's going to be a long ride into the next century. All the obstacles—the water crises, the food production crises, the destruction of the environment and the atmosphere and so on—all of these are going to be hurting every country, the big powers and the small powers. That is why it is so important that this intermediate-level civil society get busy helping to build up the capacity to take a problem-solving approach to all these new problems which most

63
.
.
.
.
.

people today don't think even exist. The challenge is not only to learn that they exist, but to take a positive attitude toward resolving them.

I'll close by saying how much I agree with carving out this middle range for attention and reminding us of what Randy said last time: The significance of government policy is that it opens a space in which people's organizations can work. That is exactly what, for example, the nuclear weapons-free zones have done.

Round Table Discussion

"This morning the U.S. Secretary of State indicated that the U.S. is ready to use force unilaterally against Iraq," Virginia Straus, BRC executive director, observed. "Would you comment, Randy?"

"The nature of the appropriate response," Randall Forsberg replied, "is affected by prior assumptions about the views and behavior of the international community with respect to acts of that kind."

"If," she continued, "we were living in a more ethically configured world, then, certainly, I would say in the case of Iraqi aggression, once the non-military means have been exhausted, and the international community has warned that military force will be used as the means of last resort to end and reverse cross-border military aggression—and if that principle were consistently applied around the world—then I think the use of force would be appropriate. However, I think it would be inappropriate for the U.S. to constitute the majority of force, let alone to decide whether or not it is time to move to military action."

"Right now, there is a lot of moral ambiguity on both sides. But in the kind of system that I'm outlining, there would be steps defined toward the abolition of weapons of mass destruction by the great powers."

"And I think," Elise Boulding added, "that the skill level of the diplomats is critically deficient at this point—particularly in the U.S. We have consistently, in effect, dared Iraq to do what it is doing. The fact that we put so few resources into training our diplomats and so much into training our weapons and military strategy specialists is ridiculous."

"It is crucial to define the non-offensive military capabilities that you would allow to exist under your proposal," Seyom Brown, Lawrence A. Wien Professor of International Cooperation at Brandeis University, said to Dr. Forsberg. "It is difficult to distinguish an offensive capability from a defensive capability. Are we, for example, ruling out attacks into the attacker's territory? And what about the establishment of some kind of intervention capability in the system? If we allow our countries to go in under a

65

multilateral mandate, aren't we still allowing them to retain capabilities which would violate your defense-only stricture?"

"And what," Virginia Mary Swain, co-director of the Center for Global Community and World Law, wondered, "do you think of the possibility that personal presidential crises (such as that which President Clinton is now experiencing) escalate unilateral responses to international crises?"

Community activist Barbara Sullivan returned to the subject of the adequacy of diplomatic training, observing that "it was incredible how ill-prepared diplomats and state department people were to work with the conflict resolution community" in a conference she had attended. "It was all power politics and what's good for this country. There was no way to bridge that gap."

"I think there's a little ambiguity," Laura Reed, visiting scholar at MIT in security studies, offered, "in terms of whether your focus is on the United States and the U.S. audience or is toward a more global agenda. In addition, the linkage between this preoccupation with traditional security concerns and the many other looming problems and issues—poverty, ecological problems, etc.—should be more strongly stated."

Carol Cohn, professor of sociology and women's studies at Bowdoin College, returned to the issue of training: "We put so much money into training people to use weapons, but we do not train people adequately in conflict resolution, mediation, and diplomacy. In whose interest would it be, what player does it require, to push the issue of diplomatic training forward? As it is now, we sometimes get the diplomatic outcomes that we want but they aren't diplomatic at all: they're military."

According to author Robert Irwin, there is a sharp dichotomy between the U.N.- and rule-of-law-centered system for international politics and the U.S.-dominated, unilateral military force-centered system.

"The U.S.," he posited, "is not only imposing economic sanctions against Iraq—and we see so little in the media about the number of people, especially children, who are dying there because of the sanctions—but the U.S. is also using economic sanctions against the U.N. by refusing to pay its dues."

"How do we build larger coalitions of NGOs—many of whom

have their own vested interests—around the broader security issues we are discussing?" Rob Eppsteiner, board member of the BRC, asked.

Seeing things differently from Randy Forsberg, Loyal Rue, professor of religion and philosophy at Luther College, took up the issue of the *homogenization of the planet.* "I agree with you, Randy, that information technology and communication technology have the potential to break down barriers between *us* and *them*, but they also have the potential to build them up. If you look at the way in which conservatives have made use of radio talk show programs, they are actually exaggerating these barriers. There is a lot of tribalization going on."

In addition, he wondered, "Are there any precedents for multilateral approaches to eliminating institutionalized behaviors (such as slavery)?"

Addressing some of the issues raised, Randy Forsberg replied, "The proposal I'm making for national defense consists solely of border guards, coast guards, and air defense systems. That's all. No retaliatory capability, no aggressive capability, no cross-border attack capability. Any ability to attack another country is relative to that country's ability to defend itself. The forces that I'm advocating as national defense forces are really extraordinarily defensive as these things go."

"In the world I'm trying to move toward," she continued, "this would be a gradual transition. Initially you would have countries contribute national components to a multilateral force except without the predominance of one country. Later you would not have national components. You would have a standing U.N. force. We need to demonstrate that the international community can provide defense and that it will not be oppressive."

"Ideally," Forsberg elaborated, "what you're trying to do is to set a standard that will frighten, deter, and teach those who might otherwise commit aggression into not doing so. The far more intractable situation is going to be to develop standards for multilateral intervention to end genocide."

"The virtue of your approach," Seyom Brown volunteered, "is that it is not simply relying on military diminution, but it is also linked with very vigorous diplomacy. That will be crucial."

67

"The potential for a major war," Dr. Forsberg insisted, "is limited to a small number of countries. One hundred and forty out of 160 countries in the world already have non-offensive defenses, and they're not capable of committing large-scale international aggression."

"Would we have humanitarian intervention for the purposes of preventing large-scale violence and genocide?" Saul Mendlovitz, professor of international law at Rutgers University, asked.

"The problem is," Forsberg responded, "that as you go down in scale, you have to weigh the rule of law internationally against national sovereignty and letting people work things out. It's very, very difficult."

"I ask," Forsberg, the IDDS founder, said to the participants, "who is the constituency to support this transformation? It is certainly not the military. It's not the foreign service. It's not the mainstream. That leaves the peace movement, and the peace movement doesn't want to do it because it means getting your hands dirty. It means taking principled positions that you don't feel confident taking. You don't want to be subverted or sucked into the war system and find yourself supporting something that ends up doing the opposite of what you had hoped and expected."

"I think you're wrong, Randy," Saul Mendlovitz responded. "The Peace Action people now are very much into this."

"The peace movement is much more diverse," Elise Boulding observed. "I think you make a good point in being explicit about what's entailed and raising the question of force."

"The formation of the U.S. Institute of Peace is not well understood," she went on. "I was on the commission that brought it into being. They have created a marvelous series of seminars that really brings a different way of thinking that is so lacking in the actual practice of diplomacy. It can be disappointing that more hasn't happened, but I think the glass is half full rather than half empty."

"With respect to global homogenization," Professor Boulding continued, "it is essential to maintain the maximum cultural and social diversity, including languages. We should be as worried about languages disappearing as we are about birds and bees and butterflies. Each culture has its own ways of dealing with conflict. The more cultures we lose, the more ways of dealing with conflict we lose."

"The other countries need to step forward as much as the United States needs to step back in order to create power-sharing," Dr. Forsberg added, as she responded to the earlier question about whether her position is global or oriented to the U.S.

"How do you deal with the whole question of countries creating alliances with each other to gang up on somebody else and to protect their own interests?" Carol Cohn asked.

"That's really what this idea of practicing is about," Forsberg answered. "You do not begin with a treaty. You do not commit yourself. You agree to follow the rules if the others agree to follow them. Unfortunately, the tremendous skepticism and fear that these steps will be abused and exploited or fail to work, prevents a consensus from coalescing around this new way of achieving security."

"Changing ideas and sharing ideas: these are difficult to achieve," Randy Forsberg concluded, "but I feel that we've reached a better understanding as a group today than we had prior to this point."

Cultural Strategies for Structural Transformation: IGOs and NGOs

BY ELISE BOULDING

Today we will begin by focusing on how states *as states* can be thought of as a possible part of the peace culture movement, and then connect these developments with the NGO world. States are the basic units of an international military system based on power relationships, but we may be in for a paradigm shift. States may move from a focus on power to a focus on relationship. We must not underestimate the possibility that we could actually change the self-image of diplomats and state leaders.

The kinds of treaties and agreements and steps toward disarmament and moving to non-offensive defense that Randy has outlined are very vulnerable to the intrusion of the power system, as we are seeing right now. All U.S. threats with respect to Iraq are undercutting relationships with other states. We are losing potential allies. The fact that the U.S. has backed NATO expansion is really undercutting the European Community's efforts to develop a new kind of relationship in Europe. And the U.S. refusal to raise the military age to 18 keeps the child-soldier phenomenon in place.

The modern state system is essentially based on a political myth, a myth of political modernization, which does not correspond to reality. The fact that we say, "All the struggles now are ethnic struggles and intrastate struggles," does not negate the fact that these are real wars. All but three of the last intrastate wars, in fact, involved major powers.

Several of us were listening to former ambassador Swanee Hunt recently, talking about women's roles in peacemaking in Bosnia. I think there we see a model of how NGOs and diplomats might carry out their missions. There are some positive signals and I want to give a positive message today. At the same time, I want to make clear how dangerous it is to continue assuming that the state system is going to survive as it now exists. Anthropologists sometimes refer to the ten thousand ethnies (cultural identity groups) spread over 185 states. Just a few of those states are mono-cultural; and 51 states have from one hundred to three thousand ethnies. The basic point I want to make here is that most states have a fair number of ethnies.

The problem that this multiplicity of ethnies creates in states is the problem of scale—the set of periphery problems that the center cannot be acquainted with. Also, there are so many different peripheries. Then there are also local terrain problems. Heads of state know very little about what is going on in the many locales within the borders of the state, and states simply do not have the kind of skills or structures that are geared to making use of local skills and local knowledge. States aren't organized that way.

The efforts to give a different role to ethnies has been part of U.N. activity and especially of UNESCO in recent years. The decade from 1988 to 1997, the World Cultural Development Decade, was set up specifically to call attention to the fact that states have all these ethnies, each with their own culture, and they need to be respected, honored, and learned from.

In the World Indigenous People's Decade, 1993 to 2003, there is an effort to get a treaty status for the three hundred million tribal peoples who have no status in international law. What I'm suggesting here is a new constitutive order based on the notion that each state is an association of ethnies. The sense of ethnic origin does not decrease over time. In fact, in the United States, more people report themselves as Native Americans now than formerly. Ethnicity is part of an individual's identity, affecting customs, language, religion.

The 1899 Peace Conference—what I will call "The Hague Tradition"—occurred at the same time that the concept of the modernized state was developing, along with the new value of states solving their problems by diplomatic means and not by military means. The possibility is that the new Hague Conference—to be held in 1999—will be a time to abolish war. There will be a parallel Citizens Peace Conference sponsored by the U.N. General Assembly. There will be discussions of a different self-image of the state.

In a new constitutive order, old borders might well stay. We're not necessarily talking about borders, although that is a big issue, too. Rather, we are talking about the status within those borders of the different constituent groups. There are large numbers of ethnies strong enough to want a degree of autonomy. This process has been going on continuously since the founding of the U.N. On the one hand, states have been founded. On the other hand, the process of negotiating for status within the state of member ethnic groups has also been ongoing.

The intense diplomatic activity involved in negotiating the status of these ethnies can be a development in the direction of peace culture at the state level. The whole point is to deal creatively with difference. If the U.S.S.R. had moved faster with its cultural autonomy programs—it was moving in this direction—we would not have had the kind of falling apart of that state we have seen. Valery Tischkov has written a lot about this process.

I want to mention some examples of the new constitutive order. Switzerland has 23 sovereign cantons and six "halves." They are still in the process of trying to figure out whether the halves are going to be separate cantons. This process has gone on since the Middle Ages. The Swiss are very proud of the fact that each canton has a degree of autonomy and sovereignty. And the Swiss people love going to the ballot box and voting. There is a very active civic process in place and Switzerland is a peaceable society.

Interesting things have been happening in Spain in recent years. Since 1979, Catalonia and Galicia and the Basque region have had autonomous status. There is still a lot of negotiation as to what that means between the government in Madrid and the people who call themselves Spanish, and these other ethnies who all have other languages as well. The process, except for a small violent faction in Basque country, is a positive one, and is still ongoing. In Catalonia autonomous status has brought a real economic and cultural flowering. The energy that autonomy has released in the province is extraordinary.

I'm very glad that my native country, Norway, has recognized an independent parliament for the Sami people. This is not a perfect solution for Sami-Norwegian relations, but there is an ongoing process, and it's been a largely peaceful one.

In Asia, Sri Lanka and Malaysia went in opposite directions, Sri Lanka giving privileges to their colonial-educated minority and Malaysia giving more opportunities to those who didn't have a colonial education. The ethnic struggles are intense in Sri Lanka and considerably less in Malaysia, where there is more of a peace process.

73
.
.
.
.
.

In the United States, there is the continuing process of the Indian peoples' treaty-making with the United States government. The struggle for casinos on Indian reservations seems to wipe out all the other news. But in the United States, the Native Americans will remind you that there are three kinds of sovereignty: federal sovereignty, state sovereignty, and Indian sovereignty.

Always this process of giving a more acceptable status to the ethnies within a country has been preceded by economic oppression of these groups. With sufficient structural recognition, people who have previously been oppressed arrive at a position where they have more freedom to organize their own social and economic development. I don't want to idealize this type of development. Nothing is ideal. All I'm saying is that in some states a creative process has evolved.

We should take note of the current move to try to get the U.N. to declare a U.N. trusteeship in Kosovo. That would be a way of dealing with a very tragic situation where the Albanians who feel like Albanians—but are in Serbia—have not been allowed to have their own schools and their own different language. The institution of U.N. trusteeship, if creatively used, could provide time and space for the development of longer-term solutions in several situations of ethnic conflict.

This reorganizing of the constitution of the modern state by giving a different status to its ethnies may be an important part of the peace process if it can change the quality of relationships and interactions. What diplomats are learning in that kind of intensive negotiation is to deal with relationship rather than with power.

I see some real promise in that. Another example of relationship-building, which I have mentioned in our earlier sessions, is the nuclear weapon peace talks and the nuclear weapon-free zones that resulted from the talks. A tremendous amount of positive problem-solving and relationship-oriented interaction has gone on to set up these treaties.

Every one of those agreements first started with NGO activity, with the initiatives of people's associations. The groundwork stayed at that level in civil society until the realms of the policymakers were penetrated. Finally came the process of the states sitting down around the table to see what they could agree to.

You can imagine how many tricky issues there are with nuclear production and the particularly tough question of what can pass through one's territory. The fact that so many zones have been agreed to shows that it is possible for people who are otherwise trained, if the context is right, to shift to this problem-solving orientation that has a strong element of establishing relationship. This is the first step in a more complete disarmament process. New habits are being developed that didn't exist before.

Each of the regional organizations—the Organization of African Unity (OAU), the Organization of Security and Cooperation in Europe (OSCE), the Organization of American States (OAS), the Association of South East Asian Nations (ASEAN)—all of these have a lot of NGO activity going on within them. Newsletters like *Terra Viva*, published by the North-South Center of the Council of Europe, help to build bridges between NGOs and the European Community. A lot of relationship-building that has much potential for peace development is taking place.

I turn now to the people's associations, the NGOs. They have their own significance in that their nature is transnational—their interests cross national borders. It may be regional interest or world interest, but these associations that I'm talking about, by definition, are not concerned with maintaining the power of a single nation-state. That's very important. NGOs have become a resource permeating the general culture. More and more they are being called on by regional intergovernmental organizations and by the U.N. itself. The U.N. couldn't get by for 24 hours without all the work that NGOs carry out in relation to the various divisions of the U.N. Here I can only give a brief overview of NGOs. Anyone wishing to know more about what I call the peace-related NGOs can check with the BRC for reprints of "Roles for NGOs in Reducing or Preventing Violence," a paper that was first presented at a conference hosted by the government of Sweden. NGOs were invited to come and discuss how they could collaborate with the government in peace-building. That is a good example of initiatives by states to reach out to NGOs.

Among the resources that NGOs bring to the conflict scene is a highly developed problem-solving capacity and a commitment that extends over the long term. State governments come and go. Often there is no continuity from one administration to another. In NGOs, however, the leadership tends to have continuity and commitment. They stay the course.

Civil society must not be overidealized. There is a real problem of accountability. This problem arises especially with transnational NGOs. These organizations don't have to report to anybody. So the need to create an accountability system, a reporting system, is very important. Several international foundations are now trying to develop a system of accountability for NGOs.

There is an interesting example in today's *New York Times* (February 13, 1998) of NGOs addressing governments. There is a full-page ad under the query, "Should Corporations Govern the World?" It's about the fact that there are 29 countries locked in secret negotiations in Paris. They are completing a new treaty that will give unprecedented power to global corporations. This ad is a very interesting example of NGOs going straight to policymakers but at the same time talking to the citizenry. Negotiators can't do anything that they wouldn't have any support for. No matter how skillful the diplomat, no diplomat can go against what is going to be supported by their government—and their country's public.

A group that I've been associated with the founding of—from the early 1960s—is the International Peace Research Association (IPRA). IPRA represents a movement to mobilize the social science community to analyze conflict in new ways and to focus on the conditions under which there can be peaceful dispute settlement among states rather than the use of military force. There are now peace research institutes in at least 70 countries. There are also about 350 peace studies teaching programs in at least 30 countries. Quite a few of them are in the United States. IPRA is an alternative to traditional international relations organizations for those who are interested in a career in international relations—whether governmental or nongovernmental. It provides a new way of analyzing the international system and introduces new concepts and new skills.

One of the important spin-offs from IPRA is the peace research regional associations. One of them, the Peace Studies Association, met here at the Center recently. Unfortunately, peace research associations have never connected well with practitioners. For some reason, there's always been a gulf between practitioners and peace researchers. I don't understand it myself. The field of professional practitioners has grown in the same period of time that the peace research field has grown, but it's grown independently.

Harvard has played an important role in that development. Now there are centers around the world where practitioners can get good professional training; some of them will be more activist-oriented advocates and some of them will be strictly impartial. There are many different roles to play in conflict situations, as I'm sure you all know. The professional associations that support practitioners are very important—everybody needs a reference group to support the way they work.

In the physical science community, Pugwash has provided a major forum for arms control discussions. We tend to forget the importance of Pugwash—that scientists from countries that have major weapon systems have been conducting intense debates and dialogues for many years now. They are a community. They have significant relationships. They are increasingly inclined to think in terms of actual responsibilities for peace-building, a shift reflected in recent newsletters.

Then there are the lawyers, including the International Association of Lawyers Against Nuclear Arms—one of the organizers of the upcoming Hague 1999 conference. There is also a relatively new Engineers Against Nuclear War. And, of course, the Physicians for Social Responsibility have been there for a long time. Each provides a public international forum for rethinking the use of armed force, and developing new norms for international relations.

In addition, there is the non-offensive defense security community, which is strongest in Europe. They, like Randy, are helping to shift the whole debate on national defense to new terrain. Each of these nongovernmental groups has their specialized capabilities; they work, as they can, with governments.

The National Summit of Africa is an example in the United States of developing—within the NGO community of African-Americans and scholars on Africa—policy positions that are directly addressed to our State Department on how to deal with conflicts in Africa.

The U.S. Institute of Peace (USIP) is a government agency that works with NGOs and must be credited with some very fine documents, seminars, and dialogues that have been held at USIP on peace-building. The Institute of Peace has no direct input into policy-making, but the fact that these dialogues are going on in Washington and that some diplomats sit in on them, makes them an important part of peace culture in the capital city.

The peace team movement started with Gandhi's *satyagraha* in India, and Peace Brigades International is one of its offspring. There are now perhaps as many as two dozen different international groups that train people in nonviolent, unarmed peace keeping. These teams are prepared to go into situations of active violence. They come entirely from within the NGO community. In situations of violence, governments are often happy to have them there, as is the U.N.

The faith-based peace movements make a very special contribution to strengthening peace culture through addressing the most difficult interreligious and interethnic conflicts in a spirit of dialogue and caring. The International Fellowship of Reconciliation, the World Conference on Religion and Peace, and the Program to Overcome Violence of the World Council of Churches all do outstanding local peacebuilding work in violent, war-torn areas.

Truth and Reconciliation Commissions represent a significant effort on the part of post-conflict governments to deal with the victims and the victimizers in situations where there has been a lot of mutual, serious damage and trauma and hurt. The seven countries I know of which have some form of ongoing commission are: South Africa, Haiti, El Salvador, Argentina, Chile, Ireland, and Rwanda. The process ideally involves moving from an acknowledgment that "Yes, I did this," and acceptance of accountability on the part of the perpetrator, to entering the empathic space of the other so that some degree of relationship and trust can be established for moving ahead into the future. When it works, genuine healing takes place

The Truth Commissions experience serious difficulty, however, when people are perfectly willing to say, as happens not infrequently, "I did so and so, and okay, I've said it, now I can go free and I'm okay." You can imagine the intense outrage of the victims in the face of that kind of an attitude. The dynamics of the commission process are still in the early stages of development. The question of how we approach the whole issue of war crimes tribunals calls for the very best energies of civil society. But the efforts of NGOs must proceed hand-in-glove with governments because it is governments which must organize and maintain the tribunals. Here is an important opportunity for serious NGO attention.

A great deal of humanitarian activity, including the work of the International Red Cross, Oxfam, and many other organizations, takes place in collaboration with the United Nations. I have visualized and written about a process of joint field peacekeeping by U.N. blue helmets and volunteers trained by the NGO community such as the Peace Brigades. Actual collaborative activity would require very different structures than we now have, but there is some movement in that direction on the part of the U.N.

Moving to the role of the women's movement in peace-making activities, I am reminded that, in an earlier session, John Montgomery felt that I had far over-emphasized that role. Women are socialized to have particular skills but this doesn't say that men can't have those skills, too. "Men can't be women," John Montgomery says. Of course not, but men can be nurturant and peaceful and very skillful at reconciliation, just as women can, and peacebuilding requires partnership between women and men. However, that is no reason not to make the most of the abilities women have due to their special socialization.

An important peacebuilding phenomenon referred to by Ambassador Swanee Hunt in a recent talk, and increasingly described in peace activist newsletters, is the phenomenon of "bringing women together." The case she was describing was in Bosnia—of bringing women together who have been hurt by each other's fathers, husbands, children. Brought together, they were able to enter into a profound relationship of empathy, entering each other's space and developing trust.

These women then go on to organize and network in their country in ways that have not yet sufficiently penetrated the highly manipulative political system which, in particular, manipulates the ethnies. What they bring to their communities are the values of conflict resolution, reconciliation, and ways of building community and dealing with difference. Their ability to accept the hurt and then move on to action is very important.

Hibaq Osman of the Center of Strategic Peace Building Initiatives for Women is helping to empower women's groups in every country in the Horn of Africa. There women are spreading out all through the region, networking country by country. In Somalia, they work with clans and sub-clans and sub-sub clans. In each case they're having to work with people who have brutalized each other's families. They have been able to weep over the brutality, hurt over it, reconcile, and move on. This extraordinary phenomenon is almost invisible. Making it visible is very important so that, at the political level, we can take account of and build on such initiatives.

Young activists and youth NGOs must also be mentioned here. Youth initiatives tend to be overlooked. The young people of the Swedish youth section of Peace Quest, present at the government-NGO conference in Sweden last year, were among the most sophisticated participants in terms of their analyses of what NGOs could do. They were with it. There was a youth assembly at the fiftieth anniversary of the signing of the U.N. Charter. They had drafted a declaration calling for a U.N. Youth Assembly and had worked out all the mechanics of how it could be done, country by country, electing delegates and so on. But they weren't allowed into the official signing ceremony. They were completely ignored. We think women are invisible: Children and youth are even more invisible.

I started out in this seminar series by saying we can't create peace at the state level if we don't have peace in our families, in our neighborhoods, in the way that we handle our problems locally; that our peace culture is an endangered species because of the high level of violence in the media and in real life, and because of the wide availability of guns. There is a lot going against the peace culture, yet it survives in fragments in every society. Our challenge is to work to reinvigorate the peace culture we have and to develop new "peaceways" at every level from the individual to the family to civil society to the state.

Systems redesign, that is, constitutive arrangements that give ethnies more space in each of their countries, is one approach to peace culture at the state level. Another is retraining for diplomats through collaboration with peace-building NGOs, with opportunities to develop problem-solving relationships rather than power relationships.

The major current peace movements like Abolition 2000, Peace Action, the Earth Charter, and all the faith-based peace movements—all of these will depend for their effectiveness on the extent to which we are empowering all the participants with peace-building skills. This must start in pre-school, with very young children. In addition to developing the skills of creatively dealing with conflict, we must all learn to understand the different levels of the systems we inhabit, from our local city hall to state government to national government to the U.N.; we must understand how our local Red Cross, Rotary, YWCA, or Scouts link to the international bodies of which they are a part. We must learn to see all the ways that we can interconnect locally with the U.N. system itself and with intergovernmental bodies as well as with international federations of NGOs.

If we don't have a mental map of the interconnections between civil society and states and ethnies and a respect for the role of each and a respect for the differences—and if we don't have the ability to open ourselves up, to empathize and enter the space of another— then we cannot create the world without war we desire.

Peace culture isn't created solely in the family; it isn't created solely in peace studies programs, or in professional and activist peace NGOs or in the faith communities, or the civil society zones of peace initiatives, or in the U.N. and UNESCO culture of peace projects. Every peace effort is interdependent with every other effort. Knowing more about that interdependence can make each of us contributors toward the further evolution of peace culture in our world.

Response

BY RANDALL FORSBERG

I'm not sure I'm the best person to be commenting on this talk. From one point of view I am and, from another, I'm not because virtually everything that Elise talked about, with one or two small exceptions, has to do with aspects of peace that I have not been working on for the last 30 years, whereas other people in the room—many other people—have been. So I'm going to make some brief comments of a few different kinds. Some of them will be questions, some of them will be challenges, and then a little free association and some connection back to what I have previously talked about, but probably the least amount of that.

This is a minor observation. It has to do with the idea of NGOs as peace-oriented. To some extent it seems to me, Elise, that you were using the idea of NGOs solely to mean NGOs which are accredited at the U.N. with the predominant interest in peace and disarmament. There is probably an equal number at the U.N. who are primarily interested in development. But then beyond those two groups there is, of course, a huge number of public interest and nonprofit organizations, many of which are very partisan and are not interested specifically in peace or development.

Then, on the other hand, many of the NGOs at the U.N. are not international. They're national NGOs who are interested in international peace. So there are a lot of cross-cutting lines, and I was reminded of that this week when I received a questionnaire. There is an association of mayors for the abolition of war which is based in Hiroshima and focuses on nuclear weapons, but not only on this. It's a thriving organization (based on the material they sent) which goes back 15 years and includes members throughout the world in very large numbers. Every four years they have a meeting. The reason that I heard from this group is that they're doing a survey of NGOs which are interested in peace and disarmament to see whether or not there's some way that they could work more closely with other NGOs for their mutual interests.

On the survey there was really no place to list your own organization, which is what they wanted to know about, if you were not an international organization, which my organization is not. So there was the question: Should I write them back and say, "I'm not the kind of organization you want to be working more closely with because we're not international. We're a domestic NGO." So you get the idea of the complexity.

I think this organization probably mailed this questionnaire to the members of the NGOs that are accredited with the U.N., which are listed in a book that we have and we put on our mailing list every year and we update, which is quite a large number. The list is publicly available. There's a kind of institutionalizing of some of the issues that you were talking about.

I couldn't help but think of the Committee on the Present Dangers as a very different kind of NGO and then there are various sorts of right-wing organizations which have some of the characteristics of NGOs but not others. Actually, I wasn't sure whether you were thinking only of the groups accredited at the U.N.

Another point, toward the end of your talk, in focusing on small children and nurturing and teaching the values that will lead to peace as people become adults: I realize that I was surprised that you hadn't said a word about capitalism since it seemed to me that when children are being taught about society, they are either taught to share or they're taught to compete. It leans in one direction or in the other direction.

The approach that I've described in the past sessions has to do with focusing on military establishments and armed forces and the military side of national policy as obstacles to lasting peace and as obstacles to the development of the values that would permit a lasting peace. My approach is very much a top-down approach, as Elise identified it, a strategic approach. I ask where the smallest amount of effort could bring about the biggest result, where the smallest number of people (given the amount of time and energy they have) can make a kind of fulcrum-like change from which could flow very massive institutional change.

Elise is presenting very much a bottom-up approach. It's hard to see it in any other way than a pyramid, this "grass" and "roots" where you've got all this grass that's growing up through the culture, penetrating the institutions and the values and the practices and the skills and so on.

I can't help but think about these two visions of what's needed for peace as being complementary, mutually important to each other, the opposite of mutually exclusive—that each one, if and to the extent that either of them is going on, would reinforce the other one and support it in a variety of direct and indirect ways. In that sense, it might be a good idea if we tried to write a book together about the conditions for peace and try to think a little bit more than I think we've succeeded so far in doing in these four sessions about the relationship between these two approaches. We might consider exactly how they bounce off each other and whether there are things that might be more effectively done on either side with respect to thinking about what's going on on the other side.

As I struggled to think about this while Elise was talking—and I had read the piece Elise gave in Sweden and also had had the benefit of looking at her outline—I was thinking: How does this relate to what I was talking about last week? There were two main thoughts that I had. The first is, how not to invite a comment I have had in our three previous sessions which is that I underestimate the amount of violence in this society or the nature of society itself.

It seems to me that there is an important quality in violence as a problem for societies, for individuals, for cultures, which makes it different from other social problems. And that important difference is that of all of the evils and burdens and unnecessary hurts that human beings suffer and inflict on each other, only violence is the quintessential *unnecessary* one where, in a sense, what we're looking for is as simple as saying "No!" to violence. *Violence is wrong and there are no exceptions.*

I feel this is a lesson that *is* learned, and *can* be learned short of the much more extensive development of participatory democracy and egalitarian institutions and empathy—short of the kinds of things that Elise is describing. It's not that they don't help, but it seems to me, there really isn't any moral ambiguity about the rule that *people shouldn't inflict violence on each other*. It's one of the very few things in life that isn't ambiguous and complex and difficult.

Generally speaking, it seems to me that the delegitimization of violence is a project of the later twentieth if not of the twenty-first century, rather than the seventeenth, eighteenth, nineteenth or early part of the twentieth century.

This notion that parents can't beat children and teachers can't beat students and husbands can't beat wives and people can't beat up on other people is part of a trend—a global, legal, and moral trend toward the greater universality of the rejection of violence in whatever form it takes. I think that that's a good thing and that it's important, and it's important not to make the achievement of peace seem so overwhelmingly difficult that you just feel like you're a drop in the ocean, when what you are, instead, is a drop in the bucket and what's out there, beyond, is the ocean. Your NGO is the bucket. I can see the idea of "Violence is wrong" permeating societies more easily than a more full-blown peace culture.

Finally, another comment which is more supportive of what Elise has been talking about than the last comment. It seems to me that both Elise and I are addressing a two-culture problem. The older two-culture problem was the humanities versus science. There is a two-culture problem now: the culture of war, violence, and self-interest versus the culture of peace, nonviolence, and sharing.

Elise talked about governments being based on power-manipulating or power-mongering. I don't really agree with that except insofar as the individuals in governments have a power-mongering cultural mindset with respect to their own personal values and their own behavior.

It is not that there aren't elements of this—particularly in the great power system—in the largest nations and particularly in their military policy and in aspects of their foreign policy. But, really, this is not all that governments do, and I don't think it's the bulk or the center of what they do any more.

I see governments as being massive, regulatory bodies which have a very important impact on economic aspects of life, including the regulation and direction of what kind of enterprises there are and how money is owned and moved around. There are lots of other things—such as the environment—that don't have to do with power or with war in the sense of war as an instrument of power.

To the extent that governments are "mongering" economic power rather than military power, I think they're very much reflecting the values and interests of the people in the society rather than diverging from them. The people who tend to rise to the top in government probably are both personally interested in the manipulation of power and also constitutionally susceptible to a political perspective in which it is assumed that such manipulation is appropriate, if not necessary. So, even if they're Democrats and even if they're liberal, there is a kind of seduction to which they are particularly susceptible. That's what I mean by the two-culture problem: The people who implement government policies can be seduced by the power-mongering mentality.

This seminar is focusing on war, the bulk of which is carved out by government officials who direct war and mandate it. My approach in looking at that problem is to try to confront those people who are in positions of power with the real issue, which is bad values about the use of force.

Elise talked about NGOs having continuity. The *realpolitik* view of the world has a tremendous amount of continuity which survives the particular administrations. But of course that's something that Elise is attributing to the nature of the state, whereas I attribute this continuity to the people who occupy positions of power.

So my approach is to try to confront not the *government* as such but the *individuals* who happen to be in positions of power at the moment with a mirror and say, "This is what you're doing, and it isn't nice. I don't like this picture. I want this other picture. The world doesn't agree with you. You are not representative; you do not represent me; you do not represent the majority. You offer a skewed presentation of national interests. These are *your* interests— these things you're calling our national interests; they're definitely not my interests. If people from the other culture were in positions of power, we would not be having this discussion."

So I do think that in that process of speaking truth to power, talking about how the world could be organized differently if the people in positions of power had different values, these two approaches of ours would be fully complementary. The much broader, richer, looser construction of peace at the "peace culture" level, the grassroots and NGO level, has to permeate the fabric of the culture in order for there to be a strategic discussion that could have any chance of promoting peace.

Round Table Discussion

"It is really interesting," Elise Boulding began, "that Randy is much more of an optimist than I am. I'm concerned about the un-developed potential of humans and how we may destroy the planet before we fix it enough."

"I see a considerable complementariness in both your positions," Winston Langley, professor of international relations and interna-tional law at the University of Massachusetts, began. "I wonder, Elise, whether you find any effort on the part of dominant ethnic or cultural groups to manage the relationships among the ethnic communities within their borders? And a question for you, Randy: Why has the culture that manipulates on behalf of war and direct physical violence had an uninterrupted ascendancy in modern times?"

"Would you spell out what you mean by empathy, Elise?" Neta Crawford, assistant professor of political science at the University of Massachusetts, inquired. "And would you, Randy, clarify your statement about *You don't have to create utopia to end war*?"

Heaping question on question, Barbara Hildt, project director of the North Essex Prevention Coalition, asked, "How do each of you interpret what the polls are telling us about the American people backing President Clinton in saying, *The only solution to Saddam Hussein and the threat he poses is to go in and take military action.* What do these polls mean in your view?"

"Yes," Elise Boulding began, "the dominant culture manages the other cultures in a multi-ethnic society. Even when they talk about giving autonomy, it's a patronizing conversation."

"With respect to empathy," she went on, "and *entering another's space,* I'm thinking of the kinds of experiences that the Somali women or the Bosnian women are having when they come together. They tell stories. The result of the storytelling is that they're enter-ing each other's spaces. Each is feeling what it's like to be the other. It's mutual. It has to be a two-way process. It's a degree beyond respect and enables people to trust each other."

"It seems to me," Neta Crawford responded, "that what you haven't addressed is the emotional relationship. When you describe what these women are doing, it is a process of dealing with the emotions in a way that is not respected by the larger male-dominated culture—the telling of stories and crying. What's ironic is that you mention *peace culture* but you neglect to speak of *culture*—of poetry, music, plays, etc. That is where the stories of people's lives are told."

Returning to the question of the polls, Professor Boulding reminded people that "the way you ask a question affects the answers you receive." She went on to say that "I do not perceive a war hysteria at all. And when it comes to ground forces, you are not going to find a lot of popular support for that."

"You provided many examples, Elise, of how the powers-that-be have been brought to the table with weaker parties and have heard what they had to say—for whatever combination of reasons—and have actually acted in a way that's different from the typical state behavior. I loved the distinction you made between looking at how to exercise power and looking at how to have a relationship," Randy Forsberg observed. "Elise, that's one of the most original things I've heard today."

"With respect to constraints on the powerful," she continued, "I'd like to use an illustration. Many of the European countries have two forms of the personal pronoun, 'You'—the private and the plural. In Sweden, as part of the social democratic revolution in the 1930s, it was required that everyone in government be addressable by their first name and by the intimate form of 'you.' This was a deliberate institutionalizing of the breaking down of hierarchy that had been very powerful in Sweden before that. This was an effort to say 'We're on a level playing field here.'"

Referring to Neta Crawford's question about empathy, Forsberg continued, "It's perfectly obvious that my shortcut, disarmament-oriented approaches have to do with these obsolete forms of warfare that probably aren't going to occur any more anyway, whereas Elise's people-oriented, one-on-one, how do you get over those deep wounds approach is, in fact, dealing with the forms of war that are occurring today and that are going to occur more and more in the future. Certainly people have to deal with very profound hurts, and respect would seem to fall a little bit short of that. I'm conceding that point. But I'd like to return to the question of Iraq. I think the international community does need to have some kind of response to a country developing weapons of mass destruction, which has used them in the past and has threatened to continue doing so, and has committed aggression against two of its neighbors within the last 20 years on a massive and blatant scale. However, it is not good that the response should be singled out on this one country."

She elaborated: "The difference between the U.S. public and the overseas public is that the overseas public sees the U.S. government directing its response at one country, unilaterally and in a partisan way. That makes people very angry about our exercise of power. The U.S. public thinks that this is an exercise of the rule of law, that the U.N. sanctions were not implemented, and that everybody else in the world is a freeloader so we must provide protection when they won't take responsibility."

"I am concerned," Saul Mendlovitz, professor of international law at Rutgers University, stated, "about the capacity for human identity and the necessity for global citizenship as it concerns ethnies throughout the world."

"The indigenous peoples all have an understanding of species identity," Elise Boulding responded, "and there's a great deal of emphasis on human identity as well as identity as a people. But I do understand your concern about people who are using ethnies for political manipulation."

Writer Eleanor Mulloney LeCain observed, "I appreciate such thoughtful discourse on some of the big issues of our time. It seems to me that what we're being fed through the media is primarily on the side of violence. We don't hear about peace studies or conflict resolution. I'm wondering what each of you would have to say about the role of the media?"

"I've attended two conferences," Professor Boulding replied, "on peace journalism and they've both been filled with stories of editors simply blue penciling the kinds of stories journalists are trying to write. Peace journalism is a weak movement at present but I think it's growing because of the dissatisfaction with the media's focus on violence.

Paula Gutlove, director of the Program on Promoting Understanding and Cooperation at the Institute for Resource and Security Studies, asked, "How do we create a paradigm where it's possible to communicate with respect and empathy? At the moment, the way international state meetings take place," she added, "there is no possibility for the kind of interaction that peace culture demands."

"I see that what you are doing," Carlotta Tyler, an international organizational development consultant said to Boulding and Forsberg, "is looking at bottom-up and top-down approaches and trying to evolve a new paradigm, a new mindset. Rather than exchanging in point-counterpoint, the two of you are coming at it more like a spiral. You're both spiraling toward one another and the dialogue is changing. You're complementary."

"I don't think it's an accident," Tyler went on, "that much of the empathetic dialogue that's been mentioned is coming from the female side of the equation, from those who have only been involved in policy-setting for about the last 50 years. The balancing that is emerging on the planet now is bringing in the voice of 'the other'— not dualistic or oppositional, but complementary."

"When people who are in war-torn countries come together," Virginia Straus, executive director of the Boston Research Center, added, "their sad stories create bonds that enable them to work together. These stories that develop empathy may be a first stage in the peace movement that can then develop into stories of transformation."

Author Robert Irwin chose to focus on metaphor. "I think about peace-making and peace-building skills and institutional structures that support them as being a system's strength. War is a breakdown in the system. I find it helpful to keep thinking in terms of stresses on a system and strength to withstand the stresses. It seems to me that we'll succeed in eliminating war when it is totally internalized in decision-makers that war is taboo."

Executive director of the Institute for Resource and Security Studies Gordon Thompson added that "humanity is in the midst of interactive transformation of culture and institutions. There's a great deal to be learned from empirical observation of how this has happened and is happening now. That could inform some discussion about how it might go in the future."

Long-term peace activist George Sommaripa interjected that "the thing that does surprise me is how difficult it is to find the peace movement. From the Fellowship of Reconciliation and the Quakers, I read about stopping exports of specific weapons and systems,

90
.
.
.
.
.

but they don't really talk broadly about peace. It seems to me that there is a lack of a crystallizing point around which people of good will can rally. I'd like to see such a point where somebody would say, 'Let's look at Pakistan and India, and at Kashmir' and say that, 'to avoid war, we need to do *a, b, c,* and *d.*' Then we'd have an organization which would try to work on the solutions. I don't see that organization yet existing, even among the NGOs."

"You're absolutely right," Elise Boulding said.

"I'm very much aware," Randy Forsberg concluded, "that you may not be able to change the institutions and the policies until you have changed the values on a much more massive scale."

"I was in Stockholm in 1972 when the first environmental conference was held there. Twenty-five years later, the whole environmental issue has changed dramatically. But the disarmament issue has not. It might be a nice idea to look at the environmental movement as an analogous sector in terms of having to change people's consciousness and public policy at all levels, from the macro to the micro, to see if there are things that have been done in that area that have not been tried in the disarmament area."

COMMENTARY

Assessing the Peace Plans before Us

BY WINSTON E. LANGLEY

Although there are important differences between the positions of Elise Boulding and Randy Forsberg, their common
goal of abolishing war cannot be realized unless both approaches
are combined.

The strength of Randy Forsberg's proposals is that they are part
of a specific plan to achieve a desired end—a plan which, to some
degree, mirrors and could strengthen the U.N.-model. That model,
exemplified in article 2 (4) of the U.N. Charter, forbids the use or
threat of the use of force by any member state against another.
The U.N. and the international community have, thus far, done
very little to have the requirements of that article implemented.
Forsberg's proposals, were they to succeed, would go far to help in
that article's implementation. Second, the proposals are timely in
that they express a widely-shared anxiety that the international
system now enjoys a favorable but brief interval within which the
Abolishing War project may be most suitably launched. But the
plan harbors some important weaknesses.

First, it does not take into consideration that the apparently
auspicious interval may be but one of the many cycles of pause
and renewal, which war—according to the various studies on the
subject, including the ongoing Correlates of War project at Michigan University—seems to observe.

Second, in its concern with the least change necessary to achieve
its laudable end, the plan leaves much of the *culture of war* intact
inasmuch as it does not provide for the new institutional structures that would assure security for all people or for the morally
transformed persons who would occupy those new institutions.
Indeed, the plan does not really rise to the level of the U.N. model
in the sense that the latter model expresses a conviction that war
can only be abolished if, in addition to limitations on the use of
force, the social, economic, and cultural privations of people are
removed. Hence, the following were established: the Economic
and Social Council and its associated institutional affiliations, in-

cluding the United Nations Educational, Scientific and Cultural Organization, the World Health Organization, and the United Nations Children's Fund.

Third, the plan commendably takes the position that there is no moral ambiguity about the rule that people should refrain from using violence against each other and that the use of force can be justified only as an act of defense. But there are ambiguities regarding what is meant by violence and defense. Violence is used to compel others to act in desired ways (or to cease acting in undesired ways). What of oppressive power which is so thoroughly established that it does not have to resort to physical force to compel others to live in conditions of wretchedness, in conditions that destroy, that violate—that is the meaning of violence—their human possibilities? And what of the *revolt* that such oppressive power invites, because some people will always insist on living authentically? What of the use of force (defense) to preserve existing structures of power in the face of such a revolt?

Finally, the plan does not tap the profound spiritual yearnings that people have for a path out of the social and moral confinement of the day—a yearning which forms part of the women's movement, the human rights movement, the ecology movement, the Earth Charter movement, and the efforts of religious leaders to elaborate a global ethic, to mention just a few of the relevant efforts. And it emphasizes mistrust (and that emphasis is very important) as the cause of war to the exclusion of cultural misperceptions, economic competition, and the wound in the cultural constitution of human beings which induces them to seek domination of others.

Elise Boulding's proposals, although not yet hewn into a developed plan, actually recognize that the culture of war can only be defeated by a culture of peace—a peace culture that would make moving to war as difficult as it now is to move to peace. Hence, she focuses on the abolition of war by way of the transformation of people's moral identity and the cultural images human beings have of themselves and of others. Those proposals also seek to ally themselves with many of the ongoing national and transnational efforts which have as their aim the removal of many, if not all, of the structures of violence and the building of human moral solidarity. Those efforts also have the goal of helping to develop the types of human

94
.
.
.
.
.

beings who will be "sensitive and empathic interpreters" across cultures, the types of persons who will build and maintain the culture of peace.

Finally, the Boulding proposals are not only "bottom-up," but they are also grounded on the image of future societies as truly inclusive and democratic. Within her democratic model, the very people who have been culturally transformed are the guarantors of peace. Elites will no longer as easily manipulate societies in determinations of when violence is to be applied and when "defense" is appropriate. Equally important, in taking a "bottom-up" approach, the plan contributes to a reduction in the structures of domination.

Wars have much to do with perceptions of self and the interest of that self (national interests). The *culture* of national interest, which finds itself so firmly planted even in our so-called multinational engagements, must be transformed into the *culture* of human interest if wars are to be abolished. Chants about democracy and multilateralism will not blind people to the arbitrary and morally disgusting character of much of the international conduct taken under those political labels. We need the combination of the Forsberg- and Boulding-type approaches to achieve that abolition. But we need one more piece to complete the project—a piece, alluded to earlier, which is missing from both plans.

Human interest, including global security, cannot fully develop and flower without the *global* institutional structures needed to nurture it. Many human rights initiatives have offered us an elementary moral and legal foundation around which to organize such institutions and fashion a global identity. And some of the movements mentioned earlier have been seeking to support and extend these initiatives. In addition, what is required is an overarching legal and *political* architecture to embody and democratically represent human interest, as well as the integrity of other life communities. The U.N., as it is presently constituted, cannot perform that function. It would have to be replaced, or substantially reformed and strengthened. The latter course of action would be more practicable and should be a central part of both plans.

The Principles of Fairness and Accountability

BY **SEYOM BROWN**

Events since the Forsberg-Boulding symposium—the nuclear weapons tests in India and Pakistan, the renewed defiance by Saddam Hussein of the U.N. inspectorate, the terrorist attacks on U.S. embassies in Tanzania and Kenya and the U.S. retaliatory strikes at suspected terrorist facilities in Afghanistan and the Sudan—have confirmed the urgency of the work these individuals are doing. A stark reality confronts the human species: The anarchic coercion-dominated system of world politics has evolved to the point where the prospects for our survival in at least a minimally healthy and decent condition are bleak. Both the Forsberg dimension (focusing on military arsenals and strategies) and the Boulding dimension (emphasizing attitudes and processes for dealing with conflict) are necessary and complementary dimensions of the larger project that should be engaging the best minds of the era—namely, devising practical programs for inhibiting and delegitimizing the use of force as political currency.

The symposium in which we have participated can serve as a model for bringing together champions of these two dimensions and melding them into a grand strategy for transforming the inherited war system.

But a third—political/legal—dimension is also needed to provide adequate flesh and fiber to the disarmament and consciousness-raising strategies developed by Forsberg and Boulding. I am talking of the enhancing and building of international processes and institutions of accountability.

The accountability principle holds that those who can substantially affect the well-being of others (particularly by doing them harm) are accountable to those whom they affect. *Civil society* norms and arrangements that generate accountability processes on the non-governmental level are important. But without official international institutions to credibly ensure such accountability, nations and subnational groups are driven (by venal temptation or desperation to defend themselves against the venal forces) to assert their interests by violent means, and neither disarmament schemes nor moral suasion will be able to prevent major conflicts of interest from escalating into coercive confrontations that, in turn, will make a mockery of arms agreements and anti-war covenants.

This third dimension of a practical strategy for reducing the role of violence in world politics, while currently out of fashion, needs to be revived and freshly energized. The current preoccupation with building an international civil society is all to the good; borrowing from the domestic experience of the United States and other relatively successful democracies, it is based on the realization that formal institutions of conflict resolution are hollow shells unless the people who utilize them have cultivated the habits of heart and mind of mutual respect, fair dealing, and empathetic compassion vis-à-vis their fellow human beings. But the formal institutionalization of the principles of fairness and accountability are also essential for tiding over conflicts that become bitter, in that they provide assurance to today's aggrieved parties that they can have another chance tomorrow to gain restitution. Such institutions are still woefully sparse and primitive on the international level, but no less essential for the evolution of a secure culture of nonviolence.

Unfortunately, it is at this level of international institution-building that the United States government has turned in the most disappointing performance under the Clinton administration—threatening, for example, to pull out of the WTO's dispute resolution arrangements if decisions do not go its way, refusing to sign the covenant against land mines, and, unconscionably, refusing to endorse the new treaty establishing a permanent international criminal tribunal.

I emphasize the international accountability dimension not to discourage work on the two dimensions of the anti-war strategy for which Randall Forsberg and Elise Boulding are providing such imaginative and energetic leadership. Indeed, it is the example of their intelligence and courage in the face of trends that too often seem to be going in the wrong direction that can inspire those of us working on the other dimension to persevere despite the current discouraging reversals.

The United Nations, Servant Leadership, and the Peacebuilding Institute

BY VIRGINIA MARY SWAIN

I am extremely grateful to the Boston Research Center for the 21st Century and to Randall Forsberg and Elise Boulding for the opportunity to participate in this series. My comments address both Elise's observation that a successful global security commission created by civil society at the United Nations has never worked and Randy's observation that a window of opportunity exists in the next 10-20 years to abolish war.

I was struck by how few references there were in this seminar to strengthening the United Nations. That to me is the main issue to be resolved in the debate between Randy and Elise. The United Nations is the only international peacemaking body of its kind. Randy's argument for a defensive security system is already incorporated in the Charter of the United Nations. Article 2 (paragraphs 3 and 4) provides that member states renounce the threat and use of force and pledge to settle their disputes by peaceful means; Articles 2(2), 25, 48, and 49 provide that members shall fulfill their obligations, carry out the decisions of the Security Council, make their armed forces available for international duty, and mutually assist one another in the collective defense. Since the U.N. has failed to live up to its charter obligations, new thinking and action are needed.

I believe a U.N. Peacebuilding Institute is needed to develop what Robert Greenleaf has called servant leadership.[1] It would build on the learnings of the Truth and Reconciliation Commissions, applying accountability, forgiveness, and reconciliation to engender a new vision of the United Nations as a body that would not use force at any level to make peace. An uncommon set of competencies describe the servant leaders—people whose actions are based on study, reflection, practice, and evaluation; who build relationships; who have moral purpose and compassion. They are nonjudgmental listeners who have spent time trying to come to terms with their own past trauma, unhealthy living patterns, atti-

98

tudes, and behaviors, so that they can take responsibility and not hurt, blame, or project their pain on others. Such spiritually aware leaders could apply techniques of reconciliation to model what such peacebuilding can offer to a world desperately entangled in the use of force to make peace.

A U.N. Peacebuilding Institute to train servant leaders would include all stakeholders of civil society to address root causes of the use of force from the personal to the global levels and to begin to build a global security commission. People who are fully conscious of the power and promise of their spiritual lineage can grow in their understanding of the role they could take globally with their unique gifts, values, and abilities. These leaders serve their followers by helping them through their transformations rather than controlling them. They have a respect for and sense of communion with the earth and an intention to use its resources rightly. Elise's Conflict Management Continuum is enhanced by the appearance of servant leaders to apply to the penultimate part of her continuum, which is transformation. The components of accountability, forgiveness, and reconciliation are essential to the work of transformation in the United Nations. Otherwise, the world will repeat the suffering and horrors of this century's wars, ethnic conflict, and the use of force as a response to terrorism. The best of our humanity is desperately needed now.

Since 1992, The Center for Global Community and World Law has been developing an organizational development process called the Peacebuilding Process of Reconciliation (PPR) to develop political will to build on the learnings of the Truth and Reconciliation Commissions. The Peacebuilding Process, which has been used at the United Nations and in local and international settings, enlarges common interest and builds global community, to build on the window of opportunity to which Randall Forsberg alluded. The PPR is designed for post-conflict peacebuilding; it provides a way to develop servant leadership by engaging people on intellectual, emotional, and spiritual levels.

The Peacebuilding Institute could use the Peacebuilding Process of Reconciliation to develop political will for a global reconciliation service. Such a service could apply accountability, forgiveness, and reconciliation to the highest ideals of a renewed United Nations. Perhaps then, servant leaders could help the U.N. become a true peacemaking body, dedicated to serve its followers, the world's peoples, by finally abolishing war.

Note

1. *On Becoming a Servant Leader: The Private Writings of Robert K. Greenleaf,* edited by Frick and Spears (Jossey Bass 1996).

Commentary

Asking Tough Questions

by Elmer N. Engstrom

There was agreement during the seminar on at least two important points: (1) that states operate within the values of their culture; and (2) that NGOs should be the primary vehicle for whatever efforts are to be made toward the abolition of war.

There was some question about whether the NGOs' primary efforts should be directed toward the states or toward cultures. Any effort to change states' policies on the use of force—"to speak truth to power," in Randy Forsberg's words—should be based as far as possible on a clear understanding of the state-culture interaction.

Apart from truisms—that most people are not violent in their individual relations, and that hardly anyone is "for war"—the signals on the state of the culture appear to be mixed, at least within the United States. While we see a growing use of conflict resolution techniques to moderate the resort to violence, we also seem to see an increase in the acceptance and use of violence.

It would be useful to have a clear reading on this cultural issue:

- Is the society's acceptance level for violence at the interpersonal or intergroup level rising, falling, or unchanging?
- What is the relation, if any, between this acceptance level and the society's attitude toward war?

Such a reading would need to have a good deal of depth and sophistication. Some work of this kind has been done in recent years by Alan Kaye (and others?). Perhaps we have some of the answers already.

It might also be useful to think about priorities among the states to which the NGOs' efforts are to be directed. The objective of abolishing war means giving up a lot of sovereignty. The U.S. seems likely to be especially intransigent on this point. Should the effort start with other powers, or must it start at the top? Or, should it be a broadside?

Making War a Thing of the Past

BY BARBARA HILDT

Nothing could be more crucial to the future of the planet and the human race than efforts to prevent war—and to prevent the waste of critically needed resources on weaponry and excessive military expenditures. Working to prevent war also means working to end the destruction of the environment from military toxins, including plutonium, the most lethal substance ever created.

There are many good reasons why wise leaders and citizens the world over should be focusing on efforts to make war a thing of the past. According to the World Games Institute, each year approximately one trillion dollars of the world's resources is spent for military purposes. With a 25 percent reduction in military spending, the nations of the world could save enough to provide clean water for all in need; provide shelter for all in need; eliminate starvation and malnutrition; provide health care for all; stop soil erosion; stop deforestation on the planet; and stabilize the world population.

Since the end of the Cold War, the U.S. has made modest reductions in its military budget to a level of about $258 billion a year. While continuing to neglect dire human and environmental problems in the U.S., last year the Republican-led Congress voted to give the Pentagon $11 billion for weapons the Pentagon didn't want. (Meanwhile, the combined military budgets of the six nations that the U.S. government identifies as potential threats total less than $17 billion.)

Because weapons production is big business, our government has encouraged arms dealers to sell their weapons almost indiscriminately abroad. Unstable governments with poor human rights records are spending limited funds on excessive arsenals rather than taking care of other needs such as education, infrastructure, and health. Naturally, U.S. weapons manufacturers are opposed to Congress passing the Arms Code of Conduct, which would restrict the free marketing of arms to potential adversaries.

We should have learned by now that politicians in Washington will continue to help those who profit from military spending until the voters become aware of the terrible cost to society of these kinds of expenditures and insist on a much smaller, yet more than adequate, military budget. As concerned citizens, we need to encourage everyone, particularly those who can speak for whole constituency groups, to tell the president and our representatives in Congress—that it is time to address the root problems of our society and the world.

The tactics of international terrorists should have taught us that the more we allow the proliferation of weapons in the world, the greater the likelihood that weapons of mass destruction will get into the hands of terrorists. National security and international security can no longer be based on building up military forces.

I strongly agree with Elise Boulding's advocacy for the development of peace cultures and teaching young people everywhere skills in nonviolent conflict resolution. Perhaps if we can nurture a generation which understands how to negotiate with its adversaries to avoid violence, we will someday have a society that will insist on the abolition of war.

Two World Orders

BY ROBERT A. IRWIN

Few people have influenced my thinking on peace strategy as much as Elise Boulding and Randy Forsberg, nor are there many whose intellect and determination I admire as much. I would enjoy detailing my many points of agreement, and some disagreements, but on balance it seems better to refer anyone interested to my *Building a Peace System*, which comments extensively on their ideas, and here make just a few points, including a contrast of world orders that stirred some interest during this seminar series.

I am less optimistic than Randy (or Jonathan Schell) about the near-term prospects for change. But I fully support Randy's current efforts. The potential for change can only be determined by pushing as hard as possible. And Randy is pushing in the right direction. Rather than maintain a rigid "stand" that never advances toward peace, pacifists should look hard at the merits of supporting the legitimacy of narrowly defined defensive military action as part of a carefully conceived strategy to end war.

The notion of shifting toward a "peace culture" has broad appeal, evidenced by proliferating conflict resolution programs in U.S. schools. But I urge close attention to the specifics of Elise's thinking. Her conception is not a dreamy world of "New Age" harmony but in important respects its opposite. She stresses the ubiquity of conflict—even between people who love each other—and the consequent indispensability of *peacemaking skills* and *energies*, applied in persistent *efforts*, "to keep human relationships from deteriorating." Perhaps the term "peace*making* culture" would communicate better what we need?

Humankind is being pulled between two world orders based on contrasting principles: one U.N.-centered, the other U.S.-centered. The first, the world of the U.N. Charter, stands ideally (though it is greatly flawed in practice) for the rule of law and the common good. The second is a world of U.S. dominance, in which Iraq's invasion of Kuwait and defiance of U.N. resolutions are said to shockingly violate the rule of law; but the U.S. may, at its sole discretion, veto dozens of resolutions, invade Grenada, bomb Libya, invade Panama, bomb Baghdad, disregard treaty obligations to move toward nuclear disarmament, mine Nicaragua's harbors, support Israel in holding captured land and attacking Lebanon at will, and wage economic warfare against Cuba (despite annual U.N. votes condemning the embargo by margins like 110 to 2). In the U.S.-centered order, global law is invoked selectively; the operative principle is "What we say goes" (George Bush)—that is, "Might makes right."

Which order can more easily be morally justified is obvious; the U.S. dons the cloak of U.N. legitimacy whenever convenient. It portrays itself as the world's leader against a few "rogue states" that "defy the will of the international community." But the main world order conflict of our time is not the U.S. and the U.N. versus rogue states and terrorists. Rather, it is between the U.S., insistent on its right to defy the U.N. and make war with impunity whenever it wishes, and the U.N. as representative of the common interest in having a lawful, warless order. A neat symmetry illustrates this viewpoint: with one hand the U.S. (which, with its U.K. partner, keeps the other veto states barely in line) strangles Iraq with economic sanctions in the name of adherence to U.N. resolutions. With the other hand it strangles the U.N. with the economic sanction of withholding legally obligatory dues and peacekeeping assessments, itself defying U.N. resolutions.

The alternatives we face can be contrasted simply: the rule of law or the rule of military force. World peace or warlordism.

How can we change U.S. behavior? The potential lies in the high-voltage gap between this behavior and what people think is right. Poll results indicate that most Americans respect the U.N. and believe their government should obey World Court decisions— even when they go against "us." People often hold contradictory views, especially on matters remote from their everyday concerns and activities, permitting a vast range of policies. This makes it crucially misleading to say that the behavior of the state mirrors the state of the culture. The difference between positive values present in U.S. culture and the policies of the U.S. is the main power resource proponents of change here possess.

Most Americans have no idea how many of their government's policies violate global law or are inconsistent with generally acknowledged human rights. (The Meiklejohn Civil Liberties Institute in

Berkeley highlights this.) We need not persuade people so much as inform them. But to do so requires engaging their attention and hearts.

The most powerful means of dramatizing information available to activists is the nonviolent direct action campaign—or, better, a series of them comprising a movement. Consider how nuclear power's expansion was stopped. Consider what was learned (and changed) regarding racism in 1960-1965 compared with the previous 95 years—or the next 30.

Changing policy through such campaigns takes time and enormous efforts. But the potential exists. The jury acquittals of protesters who, in the 1980s, invoked global law to justify interfering with aggression against Central America, and the results of requests for political asylum, on grounds of violation of universal socioeconomic rights, by the low-income Women's Alliance in eastern Massachusetts in the 1990s, both suggest this potential.

I make this bold claim. With state-of-the-art strategizing, communications, training, and actions; with financial resources within the means of progressive individuals and foundations to supply; with use of the abundant idealism and courage of the U.S. public; and with luck: a movement using nonviolent direct action campaigns as one of its key methods could transform the United States within 10 years from World Warlord-in-Chief to global citizen.

Such a transformation would tip the scales of the human future toward survival and well-being.

A child dies every 15 minutes in Iraq while I compose these words. People despair. Species go extinct. We keep hurting our ecosystem (whether irreparably, we do not know).

We are fortunate that Elise Boulding and Randy Forsberg know human beings are capable of better. They act accordingly. So should we.

Notes Toward the Abolition of War

BY GEORGE SOMMARIPA

1. The country in the world which is the *most* military-prone is the U.S.
2. The country in the world which needs a military force the *least* is the U.S. because it is:
   - defended by the Atlantic;
   - defended by the Pacific; and
   - bordered by Canada and Mexico.
3. We have not been invaded since 1815.
4. There are no countries which could attack this country militarily.

Therefore, an organization or a person should say: We do not need a military force above a simple coast guard *at all*. *No export* of military force *at all*. Call the organization THAW (Thoughtful Humans Against War) and ask for supporters to spread the word throughout the U.S., until it laps on the shores of Congress.

Many individuals for hundreds of years have lamented wars. War is a collective activity. You can ask an individual not to murder, but you can't ask an individual to stop war. However, individuals can collectively *ask the state to stop war*. You have to have individual action, and that action must be expressed through the state. *The most important way to abolish war is to create the bridge between the individual and the state.*

REFLECTIONS

Laying the Foundation for a Stable World Peace

By Randall Forsberg

With the end of the Cold War, the existence of nuclear weapons, the shrinking world, and the steady global spread of democratic institutions, the time has come for a massive campaign to end war, comparable to the nineteenth century movement to end slavery.

Recently, a coalition of religious-based peace groups, "The New Abolitionists," has come together with this goal. (Participants include Bill Price of World Peacemakers, Mary Evelyn Jegen of Pax Christie, and Glenn Stassen.) This is the right idea. What we need is a new abolition movement on a vast scale: a serious, decades-long global coalition effort by thousands of organizations and millions of individuals who systematically, persistently, and loudly press for the changes in both government policy and popular culture that are most urgently needed to help end war.

Over the past half century, concerned citizens, writers, politicians, scholars, and others have worked for peace in pieces, that is, for partial measures of arms control, arms reduction, confidence-building, peacemaking, and so on. It is fair to say that peace writ large—the abolition of war—has been the "hidden agenda" of the peace movement. The desire to prevent war and preparations for war is what motivates and unites peace activists; yet most of the time, this goal is neither stated explicitly nor pursued as a practical political objective.

Failing to pursue government policies that would move the world toward the abolition of war represents an abdication of power as well as a self-fulfilling prophecy. For if even the most committed and convinced partisans of peace believe and act as if the abolition of war is not a realistic option, then we can be sure that neither national political "leaders" nor others in society will behave as if the abolition of war is such an option. As long as we, the loyal opposition, fail to advocate military and foreign policies that have the potential to lead to a stable world peace, we leave the field of security policy to those with no such goal. And as long as we fail to debate and eventually identify steps toward the abolition of war that have the potential to command majority support in the United States and the rest of the world, efforts for peace will be blocked at the source by our own cynicism, discouragement, and lack of a sense of empowerment.

In one of our sessions, I commented that Elise's approach was "bottom up," whereas mine was "top down." But as I also underscored, my approach resembles Elise's in that both involve appeals for action on the part of grassroots groups, nongovernmental organizations, and transnational "civil society." In that sense, both are bottom-up approaches. Both rest on the view that the capacity for good and moral social action resides in the people.

Where we differ is less in the arena of action than in the goals of action, or the defined content of grassroots campaigns. What I urge is grassroots support for an overarching concept for nations, cultures, and societies around the world to systematically work to end organized armed violence. What I have proposed here is not a complex, detailed plan, but the simple idea of holding governments and sub-state actors accountable relative to a basic, widely understood moral principle of defensiveness, or defensive nonviolence: that is, violence or armed force should never be used for any purpose except to the minimum extent needed to prevent or end its use by those who have not yet accepted this principle. Among other things, a U.S. campaign organized around this principle would raise national consciousness about the existing U.S. policy of being prepared to use armed force to protect "interests," as distinct from protecting territorial integrity and sovereignty; and it would show the implications of each for U.S. military intervention, standing armed forces, and military spending—and for respect for the rule of law and the non-use of force among nations and sub-state actors in other parts of the world.

This simple idea is fleshed out in more detail in Global Action to Prevent War, a relatively detailed proposal for government and grassroots action, drafted over the past year by myself, Saul Mendlovitz, and Jonathan Dean. This proposal combines phased cutbacks in national armed forces and military action with strengthened means of peacekeeping and nonviolent conflict resolution under the auspices of the U.N. or strengthened regional counterparts, such as the Organization for Security and Cooperation in Europe.

Hearing Elise Boulding's perspective during this series has been, as I hoped, enriching and thought-provoking. Elise's work brings home the myriad activities that energetic people in local communities and in smaller and less militarily-armed countries around the world can do to lay the foundation for a stable world peace.

The suggestions in the discussions and in the participant responses are also useful. Barbara Hildt and George Sommaripa remind us of the leading role of the United States in wasting resources and clinging to interventionist policies. Seyom Brown and Virginia Swain identify important "post-war" components of an enduring peace: institutions for holding individuals accountable for war crimes and institutions for reconciliation and rebuilding.

Winston Langley and others correctly point out that my proposal for a defensively-oriented international security system contains little that is not already established in the Charter of the United Nations; but, as Winston observes, a reconfiguration of the same basic ideas can add new energy to implementing and reinforcing moral norms that are not yet political norms.

Bob Irwin—who rewarded my hopes by arguing that peace activists should consider the norm of defensive nonviolence—made what is probably the most daringly optimistic of all of our predictions: a large, well-organized campaign of nonviolent direct action could put the abolition of war front and center on the agenda of the United States and the world within a decade.

This sharing of ideas, hopes, and doubts, like the meetings of the New Abolitionists and others, represents an early bud in what should become a long, fruitful season of brain-storming, debating, and striving. From this we will reap a global movement to end war.

Toward a More Peaceful Twenty-First Century

BY ELISE BOULDING

O ur dialogue and discussions during the *Abolishing War* seminars have given me a valuable opportunity to think through more clearly the interaction between governments and the peoples' associations we refer to as NGOs, particularly in relation to the abolition of war. Randy's strategy of focusing on government policy, because this offers maximum leverage for the amount of effort put forth, and my focus on the more diffuse civil society as the only source of the values, attitudes, and behaviors that can lead governments to adopt disarmament measures are (as we kept acknowledging) complementary. But as I read over the text of our discussions, I felt we did not sufficiently explore the interpenetration of government and civil society. The delegitimization of war that Randy counts on as the basis for more effective disarmament treaties—to the extent that the delegitimization is actually happening—is a product of value change in the civil society.

Intense, purposive focusing on disarmament at the peace movement level is, as Winston Langley points out, a cyclic phenomenon. The peace movement has, indeed, been in a trough in recent years but this has, in fact, been a period of preparation for a new peak. We are now facing a new energy surge in the peace movement, directed to very specific changes in military policy. This surge I myself was not sufficiently aware of during our seminar series. Both the upcoming 1999 Hague Appeal for Peace Conference and Abolition 2000 were mentioned in our discussions, but only recently have I been examining the actual dynamics of Year 2000 preparatory activity.

The Hague Appeal for Peace is a coalition of six hundred NGOs, many of whom are preparing substantial documentation for the Hague event. There is also a careful process of coordination occurring related to the planning for the intergovernmental Hague Assembly, which will convene concurrently with the Peace Appeal group. The disarmament proposals that are being prepared by the six hundred-strong NGO coalition will be placed directly before the intergovernmental conference.

Abolition 2000 is a loose coalition of one thousand NGOs on six continents that calls itself a Global Network to Eliminate Nuclear Weapons. While the action focus is on getting agreement on the abolition of nuclear weapons by the year 2000, a number of constituent groups, such as the International Network of Engineers and Social Scientists for Global Responsibility, are preparing detailed models of treaty agreements that take into account the entire history of arms control and disarmament agreements from 1959 on. The need for a step-by-step process is well understood. These NGOs are prepared for the long haul. The transnational NGOs have representatives at the U.N. in New York and Geneva and at all Disarmament Commission meetings, both general and special-purpose. Some of them, like the Women's International League for Peace and Freedom (WILPF), have been working since the World War I era on model covenants and treaties. WILPF had input into the 1925 Geneva Protocol against the use of chemical and bacteriological weapons. Every one of the 32 arms control and disarmament agreements that have been negotiated since 1925 has had substantial NGO involvement, often representing a level of legal and scientific expertise beyond that of the government ministries and staff responsible for the drafting of the agreements.

It is also true that over the decades there has been a steady trickle of peace activists involved in these treaty campaigns into national governments and into the U.N., where they bring the perspectives and experience gained from NGO work to the actual governmental and intergovernmental policy processes. That resource should not be underestimated.

The year 2000 is of course a pure calendric artifact. While the sense of hope and expectation of change for the better which characterized the millennialist movements in Europe in the late 900s is, in one sense, reappearing in the 1990s, this time around it is based on a more solid and informed infrastucture of peoples' associations that can translate profound human longings into workable steps toward a more peaceful twenty-first century.

Jubilee 2000, a coalition of NGOs for debt forgiveness for poor states in the biblical tradition of 51 cycles of debt forgiveness, and

Earth Charter 2000, a peoples' treaty intended to persuade the U.N. General Assembly to adopt the International Covenant on Environment and Development, are among other coalitions forming to place specific policy proposals before the U.N. General Assembly in 2000. The Year 2000 Assembly has already been declared by the U.N. a Millennial Assembly, to be followed by a Decade of Education for Nonviolence and a Culture of Peace. It makes very good sense for all peoples' associations—grassroots, national, and transnational—to make the most of this opportunity to mobilize hope, reflection, and action to end war.

Certainly not all NGOs have the skills referred to here. The development of NGO accountability still has a way to go. There is, however, a new capacity for building workable global coalitions for specific policy change. It should be noted that the international women's movement has done its part in the development of those coalition-building skills during its decades of work with the U.N. and national governments on human rights for women as well as men. The women's super-coalition, the Huairou Commission, will be right there at the U.N. Millennial Assembly, with all the disarmament, environment, and development coalitions, in a mutual strengthening process. An important function of all these coalitions is to remind governments that there is a lot of nitty-gritty "housework" to be done—locally, nationally, and globally—to achieve a twenty-first century good for humans and all living things. I would like to think we helped that process along in our seminars, and I want to say "Thank you" to everyone who participated.

PRESENTERS

Photograph by Jonathan Wilson

RANDALL CAROLINE FORSBERG is the founder and director of
the Cambridge-based Institute for Defense and Disarmament Studies (IDDS), a nonprofit center for research and education on ways
to minimize the risk of war, reduce the burden of military spending, and promote democratic institutions. Dr. Forsberg is also a
recipient of the Boston Research Center's 1997 Global Citizen Award
for her work in forging a broad-based citizens' movement for peace
and disarmament.

Starting in 1968, Dr. Forsberg worked at the Stockholm International Peace Research Institute (SIPRI) where she was the
assistant editor of the first *SIPRI Yearbook of World Armaments and
Disarmament* and a contributing author of the next ten editions.

In 1980, Dr. Forsberg wrote the "Call to Halt the Nuclear Arms
Race," the four-page manifesto of the U.S. Nuclear Weapons Freeze
Campaign, and she helped lead the campaign.

Dr. Forsberg has received a five-year MacArthur Foundation
Fellowship and honorary doctorates from the University of Notre
Dame and Governors State University. She has a B.A. from
Columbia University and a Ph.D. from MIT.

Among numerous publications, including articles in *Scientific
American, International Security, Technology Review*, and *The Bulle-
tin of Atomic Scientists*, she has edited and co-authored three books
published by MIT Press: *The Arms Production Dilemma: Contrac-
tion and Restraint in the World Combat Aircraft Industry* (1994);
Nonproliferation Primer (1995); and *Arms Control in an Era of Cooperation: Linked Restraints on Arms Deployment, Production, and
Trade* (forthcoming 1998).

Photograph by Jonathan Wilson

ELISE BOULDING is professor emerita of sociology at Dartmouth College and former secretary-general of the International Peace Research Association. She was nominated for the Nobel Peace Prize in 1990. She is also a recipient of the Boston Research Center's 1995 Global Citizen Award for outstanding contributions to international peace research and humanistic education. Dr. Boulding has also taught at the University of Colorado at Boulder.

She has undertaken numerous transnational and comparative cross-national studies on conflict and peace, development, and women in society, and has served on the board of the United Nations University, the International Jury of the UNESCO Prize for Peace, and the Congressional Commission that led to the establishment by Congress of a U.S. Peace Institute.

Elise Boulding received her Ph.D. from the University of Michigan. A futurist, Dr. Boulding has conducted workshops on "Imaging a World without War."

Among her publications are: *Children's Rights and the Wheel of Life* (1979); *Building a Global Civic Culture: Education for an Interdependent World* (1990); *One Small Plot of Heaven, Reflections of a Quaker Sociologist on Family Life* (1989); *Underside of History: A View of Women Through Time* (1992); and with Kenneth Boulding, *The Future: Images and Processes* (1994). She is currently writing a book on the Culture of Peace.

DISCUSSANTS

EILEEN BABBITT is assistant professor of international politics and director of the International Negotiation and Conflict Resolution Program at the Fletcher School of Law and Diplomacy at Tufts University. She is also an associate of the Program on Negotiation at the Harvard Law School. As a facilitator and trainer, she has worked in the Middle East, Southeastern Europe, and the Horn of Africa. Her current research interests include preventive diplomacy, post-conflict peacebuilding, and roles for third parties in protracted intergroup conflicts.

SEYOM BROWN is the Lawrence A. Wien Professor of International Cooperation at Brandeis University. He has also held senior research positions at the RAND Corporation, the Brookings Institution, and the Carnegie Endowment for International Peace. He is the author of *New Forces, Old Forces, and the Future of World Politics; The Causes and Prevention of War;* and *The Faces of Power: Constancy and Change in United States Foreign Policy From Truman to Clinton.*

CAROL COHN teaches sociology and women's studies at Bowdoin College in Brunswick, Maine. This year, while on sabbatical, she is a research associate at the Five College Women's Studies Research Center at Mount Holyoke College. Her research and writing explore the ways in which gender as a symbolic system shapes national security policies and practices. Her most recent article, "Gays in the Military: Texts and Subtexts," appears in *The Man Question in International Relations*, ed. Jane Parpart and Marysia Zalewski.

NETA CRAWFORD is an assistant professor of political science at the University of Massachusetts Amherst. She is an anti-militarist activist and the author of several articles for popular journals and a book, *Soviet Military Aircraft.* Neta is co-editor of *How Sanctions Work: South Africa* (forthcoming: St. Martin's/Macmillan). Her current book project is titled *The Making of World Politics: Argument, Belief, and Culture.* Most recently, she finished the article, "Postmodern Ethics and the Critical Challenge."

ELMER ENGSTROM, a retired business consultant, has worked on a volunteer basis at the Institute for Defense and Disarmament Studies for 12 years. He is currently contributing to a detailed study of trends in U.S. military spending since 1980.

ROBERT EPPSTEINER is vice president of the Boston Research Center for the 21st Century. He is also a representative to the United Nations and director of academic affairs for Soka Gakkai International-USA, a lay Buddhist organization dedicated to promoting peace, culture, and education. Mr. Eppsteiner has been active in peace, human rights, and environmental issues for 30 years.

PAULA GUTLOVE is the director of the Program on Promoting Understanding and Cooperation at the Institute for Resource and Security Studies in Cambridge. She is also program manager of the Program on Democracy Building in Slovakia at the Center for Strategic and International Studies. Paula initiated the Balkans Peace Project with a group of colleagues in 1991 to promote the use of conflict resolution processes that can contribute to a sustainable peace in the former Yugoslavia.

BARBARA HILDT has been a teacher, a Peace Corps volunteer in Brazil, state representative to the Massachusetts Legislature, a candidate for the U.S. Congress, coordinator of the Violence Prevention Working Group, a lecturer at the Radcliffe Seminars Management Program, coordinator of *Words, Not Weapons*, and is currently the project director of the North Essex Prevention Coalition. She is also the president of WAND. She has organized and developed programs which prevent abuse and violence and promote healthy communities.

ROBERT A. IRWIN is co-author of *Why Nonviolence? Nonviolence Theory and Strategy for the Anti-Nuclear Movement;* has served as an expert witness in civil disobedience trials; and has written *Building a Peace System*, a comprehensive introduction to world governance, alternative security, and ecological, economic, and cultural issues. This text can be used as a manual for organizing grassroots study groups.

WINSTON LANGLEY is professor of international relations and international law at the University of Massachusetts Boston and is vice president of the United Nations Association of Greater Boston. He has written extensively on U.N. operations and structure, especially as they relate to the economic, social, and legal rights of citizens of developing countries. His books include *Human Rights: The Major Global Instruments* and *Women's Rights in International Documents: A Source Book with Commentary.*

ELEANOR MULLONEY LECAIN is a speaker, writer, and consultant on transforming ourselves and our country. She has been the Massachusetts assistant secretary of state for strategic planning and executive director of Blueprint 2000. Boston Edison hired Ms. LeCain to lead a team to develop the next generation of energy efficiency programs. She has been published in *The New York Times*, the *Boston Business Journal,* and other prominent periodicals. Presently, she is writing a book, *What's Working in America.*

SAUL MENDLOVITZ is Dag Hammarskjold Professor of International Law, Peace and World Order Studies at Rutgers University Law School, Newark, and the founder and co-director of the World Order Models Project in New York City (formerly based at the Institute for World Order), a joint international project of social scientists from all continents with the goal of sketching the shape of substantially different, preferable futures.

JOHN MONTGOMERY is the Ford Foundation Professor of International Studies Emeritus at Harvard University. He has initiated interdisciplinary approaches to policy research and administration in Pacific Basin countries and is now the director of the Pacific Basin Research Center. He is currently working on Positive Human Rights policies and is designing a study program on peace movements in Asia.

KAREN NARDELLA is program manager at the Boston Research Center for the 21st Century and coordinator of the *Abolishing War* seminars. Trained as a journalist, her professional experience is in media, advertising, and communications.

LAURA REED is a visiting scholar at MIT in security studies and a contributing editor to the first annual Institute for Defense and Disarmament's *World Survey of Arms and Arms Control* (forthcoming 1998). As a fellow at the American Academy of Arts and Sciences she co-edited three books: *Collective Responses to Regional Problems; Emerging Norms of Justified Intervention;* and *Lethal Commerce: the Global Trade in Small Arms and Light Weapons.* In 1996-1997, she co-authored *The State of the Art: Human Security and Global Governance* (forthcoming).

LOYAL RUE is professor of religion and philosophy at Luther College in Iowa and served during 1997-98 as a senior fellow at the Harvard Center for the Study of World Religions. At Luther, Professor Rue has chaired the International Studies Committee and also the Environmental Studies Committee. He authored Luther's academic program in environmental studies. He is currently working on his fifth book which examines the role of religious traditions in expanding human capacities for global solidarity and cooperation.

APPU SOMAN holds a Ph.D. in diplomacy history from Vanderbilt University. He has written extensively on the conflicts in Asia between India and Pakistan, China and India, and China and the U.S.

GEORGE AND EVA SOMMARIPA. George was a founding member of the Institute for Defense and Disarmament Studies and served as its treasurer for many years. He is a life-long peace activist, knowledgeable about defense spending and peace activities. Eva, a certified organic farmer who has long been interested in and worked for world peace, represented her husband at the seminar series when George became ill.

VIRGINIA STRAUS is executive director of the Boston Research Center for the 21st Century. She is a public policy specialist who formerly directed the Pioneer Institute, a state and local policy institute in Boston which she helped to establish in 1987. She also worked for nine years in Washington, D.C., serving as a legislative researcher in the House of Representatives, as a financial analyst in the Treasury Department, and finally as an urban policy aide in the Carter White House.

BARBARA SULLIVAN is a community activist who has been involved in environmental, human services, and peace advocacy since the 1960s. She has served on the board of several organizations including the Consortium on Peace Research, Education, and Development (COPRED), and was coordinator of the Conflict Resolution Section of that organization for three years. She is currently retired from the Massachusetts Department of Mental Health after 20 years in Child/Adolescent Services.

VIRGINIA SWAIN has been an organizational consultant and seminar leader in the United States and abroad since 1986. She specializes in conflict resolution, team and community building, and change management for individuals and groups. She is a co-founder of the Cambridge-based Center for Global Community and World Law and is a principal of The Center for Strategic Change. Virginia was a Peace Corps volunteer teacher in West Africa, and she is the co-author of *The Way of Peace: How One Person Can Make a Difference Toward World Peace.*

GORDON THOMPSON is executive director of the Institute for Resource and Security Studies, Cambridge, Massachusetts, and coordinates the Institute's Proliferation Reform Project. He was educated in science and engineering in his native Australia and obtained a doctorate in applied mathematics from Oxford University in 1973. Since then, he has pursued a wide-ranging career as a scientific consultant on energy, environment, sustainable development, and international security issues. For the last 11 years he has been based in the United States.

MICHAEL TRUE is convener of the Nonviolence Commission of the International Peace Research Association and author, most recently, of *An Energy Field More Intense Than War: The Nonviolent Tradition and American Literature* (1995). Recently retired from Assumption College, he was a visiting professor at Colorado College, University of Hawaii, and Nanjing University. In 1998, as a Fulbright scholar in India, he is lecturing on American literature at Utkal University, Bhubaneswar, and on nonviolence at the Centre for Gandhian Studies, University of Rajasthan, Jaipur.

123
.
.
.
.

CARLOTTA TYLER is an international organization development consultant to clients in corporate, academic, government agency, and non-profit sectors in North America, Europe, Australia, and Pacific Rim countries. She is a former director of marketing for a computer manufacturer, a former elected political leader, and a small business entrepreneur. Currently she is serving her second term on the national board of WAND.